THESE

DREAMS

OF

YOU

These Dreams of You

Ann McCloskey

GREEN WRITERS PRESS
Brattleboro, Vermont

Printed in the United States

10 9 8 7 6 5 4 3 2 1

Green Writers Press is a Vermont-based publisher whose mission is to spread a message of hope and renewal through the words and images we publish. Throughout we will adhere to our commitment to preserving and protecting the natural resources of the earth. To that end, a percentage of our proceeds will be donated to environmental and social-activist groups. Green Writers Press gratefully acknowledges support from individual donors, friends, and readers to help support the environment and our publishing initiative. Green Place Books curates books that tell literary and compelling stories with a focus on writing about place—these books are more personal stories/memoir and biographies.

Giving Voice to Writers & Artists Who Will Make the World a Better Place
Green Writers Press | Brattleboro, Vermont
www.greenwriterspress.com

ISBN: 979-8-9870707-3-4

PRINTED ON PAPER WITH PULP THAT COMES FROM FSC-CERTIFIED FORESTS, MANAGED FORESTS THAT GUARANTEE RESPONSIBLE ENVIRONMENTAL, SOCIAL, AND ECONOMIC PRACTICES.

For Caitlin

"In my next life I want you to be my mom again."

—Colleen McCloskey-Meyer, age 4

CONTENTS

Prologue

NOVEMBER 28, 2017

I AM STANDING IN MY KITCHEN, with my back to the stove, facing into the open dining area. The door to outside is across from me. People are beginning to leave. There have been so many of them: first responders, police officers and a detective, a social worker, a death examiner, two people from a funeral home. So many vehicles outside that some are parked on the lawn. Why did we call 911 anyway? We clearly didn't know what to do, and this call has led to so much unnecessary chaos. The police officers, one of whom went to school with our daughter Colleen (and who has told me this afternoon that he remembers her as "very smart"), approach me to offer their condolences, one by one. They look me in the eye. They have been well-taught. I am struck by this, despite my eagerness for these many interlopers to vacate my home. They seem kind. I know that I am experiencing some emotional numbness in their presence, and I want them to leave so I can be alone. I am tired, so tired, and I want them all gone. I want to be alone with my husband so we can face what comes next.

I hear sounds coming from the stairs. I have been told that Colleen's body will be taken out in a sling, rather than on a stretcher. She is so tiny, weighing just forty-four pounds, despite being a full grown twenty-seven-year-old woman. She has died from anorexia, which has been with her since she was just ten years old. So, a sling will be easier. I have agreed to this. It makes sense. An ambulance driver and someone else maneuver the sling around the corner at the base of the stairs and through the dining room and kitchen. Colleen's body is so small that I cannot see her in there. I cannot see her long hair, her face, her beautiful blue eyes, any part of her. There is just a suggestion of her shape and weight in that sling. But the suggestion is strong. Her lifeless body is going out the door in a sling.

I begin to crumble. I start to weep. I back up against the stove as far as I can go. I just want to be alone. Or is it that I want to disappear? This is too much. It has all been too much, and this is now completely too much.

The woman from the funeral home, with whom I have talked in my living room this afternoon, approaches me, and offers a hug. She leans in, and her embrace is warm. This hug is brief, which is good, and then she follows the others out.

And that's it. Colleen is gone. She came home late last night to die here with her father and me by her side. Her death has been expected, yet it has been heart-wrenching for us to witness. We understand it has been important to all of us that she leave this world while we hold her hands. But we brought her into this world, and to watch her go out at such a young age has been devastating. Colleen struggled to breathe for twenty long minutes from deep inside her diabetic coma this afternoon. I spoke to her throughout that time, reminding her that it was OK to go, that we loved her, and that this last difficult bit would be over soon. Now it is over. Her struggles, her short life, all of it. She is gone from us, and the next phase of our lives begins.

And I think, as I stand against this stove, that there will always be a before and after, before Colleen's death, and after it. The after begins on this bleak day in late November as her body is taken out in a sling.

THESE

DREAMS

OF

YOU

1

January 2001

"Is SHE DEPRESSED?" asked my friend Sally over the telephone.

"Yes," I responded, "But first came the obsessive-compulsive symptoms, then anorexia, and now depression. She is depressed because she is starving."

"Right," said Sally. She understood this. It was good to be talking to someone who I did not need to explain everything to. Sally is, as I was back then, a psychotherapist.

I had been searching for weeks for a therapist to work with my daughter, who had been losing weight very rapidly. She was just ten years old. No one in the tri-state area was willing to touch this. Therapists I contacted worked with teens with eating disorders, or they worked with children, but they all seemed afraid to go near a child with an eating disorder.

Colleen had been restricting her food intake, gradually, for a few months, but she had been secretive about this, and I had missed it entirely until very recently. I had thought her body was simply changing in that pre-pubescent way that girls' bodies do. And then, just after Christmas, I noticed how little she was eating and how thin she had become, seemingly overnight. I talked to her about this, of course, but I was met with denial. I made an appointment to talk with her fifth-grade teacher when school resumed after the holiday break. Her teacher confirmed that Colleen had been eating very little at school, but she said she had been hesitant to say anything to me. I was incredulous to hear this. What was she worried about? That I might disagree with her assessment? She was more concerned with my reaction than with the fact that a child was not eating her food?

Now I was spending most of my waking hours looking for help for my daughter, while also talking with Colleen about what she was doing and trying to talk sense into her. She was conflicted. She told me this. After days of conversation, she thought maybe she should eat more, but she also thought she should not. I knew she needed to talk to someone other than me, but I couldn't find anyone to take this on. I was well-connected in the field of psychotherapy, and I had many people helping me search for a clinician, yet I continued to end each day with nothing more than I started with.

I was tired. I was sleepless. I had two half-time jobs and a five-year-old daughter as well. I taught in a graduate program, and I worked as a clinician at an elementary school. My coworkers at the university where I taught were supportive. They had suggestions. Nothing panned out. I was late for work at my school job one morning, late for the first appointment of my day with a young boy who had little consistency in his life. He was angry when I got to his classroom to collect him for what would be our abbreviated time together. I felt bad about this, but my daughter had refused to eat her breakfast and she was wasting away.

I was at home one afternoon with my five-year-old, Caitlin. We were in her bedroom, and she was playing with her dolls. I often played with her, but this day I was distracted. Very distracted. Caitlin said to me, "Mommy, why don't you ever play?" I felt terrible about this. I felt terrible that she had come to see me as someone who never played. Her experience of me was that I was no fun. I used to be fun, but she did not seem to remember this. I was letting many people down, as I struggled to save one child, my daughter who was starving.

I spoke with the school nurse, who agreed to weigh Colleen and check her vital signs every other day. Nurse Jane reported to me. It would have been much better if she could have reported to a therapist, but I couldn't find one.

It appeared that Colleen was eating less every day. I made her the snacks she liked after school; she took them to her bedroom and reported that she had eaten them. I didn't know if this was true. I wanted to believe her. She had never lied to us before, but now I didn't know. She was continuing to lose weight, and she was becoming more and more distracted. Her usual sharp focus on whatever was happening in her presence was no longer a constant. She seemed to be in her own world much of the time.

Tuesday, January 30th, was a frigid, icy day, but school was in session, and I was headed to Keene, New Hampshire to teach my students. I was terrified that Colleen was going to slip away before I could get her the help she needed. She was consistently one step ahead of me with this thing she was doing. My good girl who always told me everything was lying to me and to her dad. She was lying and cheating in her desperation to be as thin as she could be. She was suffering from mental illness. This had all happened so quickly, and I was working so hard to keep up. I was falling behind. She was winning this crazy battle. I knew I had to do something else, but I didn't know what that could be. I began thinking about having her admitted to a hospital. I didn't want to overreact, but I thought we could be headed in this direction. I really wanted help with this; a therapist to meet with her and then with me would be great, but when was I going to find someone willing to take this on?

I arrived at work in time to teach my first class. I would later remember little about the teaching I did. On the break between my classes, I called our family physician, Richard. I told him what had been going on, and he told me to call the school and get Nurse Jane to pull Colleen from class and check her vitals again, now, even though this had been done the day before, and to tell Jane to call him. It felt like a long time before Richard called me back, but it was not. I had just a half hour break between classes and that break was not yet over. He said I should bring her in. I cancelled my second class and headed back to Vermont from where I taught in New Hampshire, to get Colleen from school. The roads were very icy, forcing me to drive slowly. When I finally arrived, the school day was over, and Colleen was waiting for me. She was to go somewhere else after school that day, perhaps to dance class, perhaps to her grandmother's house, but plans had changed. She had been told to wait for me. She was resistant to this change to her afternoon, but she was just ten and she had no choice in this matter.

The trip north to Richard's office took longer than the usual twenty minutes. The treacherous driving conditions called for my full attention, yet Colleen's anxiety was palpable.

"What are you thinking, honey?" I asked.

"I don't know. I don't know what's happening."

"You look a little nervous and scared. Are you feeling scared?"

"I don't know. I don't know anymore. I really don't want to eat, but you are making me scared about not eating. You are making me feel scared. Why do we have to see a doctor? Can't I decide what to do?"

"It's your safety I'm concerned about, Colleen. Remember talking about this yesterday? You're eating too little to stay alive. You could die eating this little. And I know you've thought a lot about the idea of turning this around, but you haven't made a change and you're losing weight so fast. I am worried about you. I love you and I need you to keep living. Dad and Caitlin love you. We all need you. We need you to stay alive. And I think you want to stay alive."

Tears rolled down Colleen's face. She seemed especially affected by my mention of her little sister, Caitlin. "Caitlin needs you, Colleen," I repeated. This seemed to be the hook, at this moment anyway. This felt like a win to me. If Richard were to suggest hospitalization, that would be the path we would follow, but it would be so much better if Colleen could agree with this decision.

"I know this is scary, honey. I know it is. You're being very brave. You're a strong and brave girl, and we are going to get through this together. OK?"

"OK," she sniffed, in a small weak voice. She looked so small sitting there. She was so small; her body had become tiny. Colleen's usual gutsiness seemed replaced in this moment by compliance. She had become exhausted and weak, both physically and emotionally. *Compliance is good right now,* I thought. *This is exactly what is needed. This is a win. This is going to work. I am finally going to get her some help. I have got this. We have got this.*

We talked with Richard when we arrived. He asked both of us many questions. Colleen answered honestly. It was clear that she was still conflicted, but beginning to cooperate nonetheless. She had been hell bent on becoming as thin as she could, but she was also young enough to feel alarmed by the level of concern among the adults in her life. Richard left the room to call our local psychiatric hospital to see if they had a bed. Colleen appeared to be scared. I asked her if she wanted to sit on my lap. This was something she had not done in years and would never do again; she was ten after all. But she was nervous about going into a hospital, not at all sure that she wanted to do this. She moved over to sit with me. Richard returned to say that there was no bed that night but that there would be one available the next day, and I should call the hospital in the morning. So we headed home to West Brattleboro.

When we arrived at our road, Bear Hill was too icy for my car to climb it. We left the car at the bottom of the hill and walked up, not on the slick, icy road, but in the crusty snowy stuff alongside the road, in the dark. It was rough going and Colleen fell behind, slowly trudging up the hill. I was afraid for her. I was afraid she would fall and break a bone. I was afraid her heart would give out. I told myself that she had not been starving long enough for these catastrophes to occur, but I wasn't sure that was true.

I don't remember much about that evening. I know that Colleen ate nothing, but I don't recall how we passed the time. I do know that she went to bed early, exhausted, and that she asked me to hang up her clothes as she dropped into bed. She had dropped them onto the floor in her exhaustion. She was tired; she had so little strength left from not eating for so many days and from that grueling trek up our road. Neither Joe nor I slept that night. We quietly took turns going in to check on Colleen, making sure that she was breathing.

In the morning I called the psychiatric hospital in our town to confirm our appointment, and I was told that Colleen would need to go through the emergency mental health system to be admitted. We would have to take her to the Emergency Department at the local hospital to have her assessed by the on-call mental health clinician. We decided that Joe would take Caitlin to preschool, and I would take Colleen to the hospital. But first I called the agency I worked for as a school-based clinician, the agency that provided these emergency assessments. We arranged a meeting at a pediatrician's office instead of at the hospital, the office of a doctor I knew professionally as well. I called my boss, Diane, at the university where I taught, to say I would not be in. She asked me for the time and place of this meeting, which was to happen just thirty minutes later, and she said she would be there, although she was at least thirty minutes away. And when Colleen and I arrived, there she was. And there she stayed, by my side, all day long. It was a long day.

It was evening, well into the evening, when I drove home alone from the hospital. Diane had left us in the late afternoon, before we got as far as the psych hospital, but after many hoops had been jumped through. She had been immensely helpful to me in navigating this process; Diane had raised a son with bipolar disorder and had seen him through many hospital admissions. In her wisdom as a psychologist, Diane had reminded me midday, while we waited outside the library for Colleen to return a book, that Colleen had a thought disorder. I knew Colleen was not thinking in a normal way, but in my exasperation, I had briefly lost sight of this. Diane had been helpful earlier in the day as well, when in an interview she remembered a detail about Colleen's behavior I had forgotten to report. It is very helpful to have psychotherapists for friends when you are frazzled and exhausted, in the midst of dealing with a mental health crisis.

I wound my way through the empty streets of our town on that cold, silent, late January night. My daughter was safe; she was in a psychiatric hospital. She had never been away from home, except for an occasional sleepover at a friend's house. But there she was, in a psych unit with mostly teenagers; the hospital did not have a children's unit at that time. I was exhausted and relieved and a bit scared for her, as I drove slowly through snow-covered neighborhoods, no longer in a rush, no longer racing to keep up with my daughter, a step behind her all along. It had taken a month, but I had finally found help for my starving daughter. My ten-year-old, who had recently told me that she had never heard of anorexia when she had decided to get as skinny as she could.

2

These Dreams of You:
On Your Birthday

May 14, 2022
Dear Colleen,

Your birthday is always such a glorious day, just as it was the year you were born. Pink and white blossoms, spring green leaves. Your crabapple tree is blooming nicely this year; mine seems to be taking a year off. But still their branches entwine so gracefully as they put on that spring green show together.

You would be thirty-two today, Colleen. You have been gone four and a half years. I am writing about you and me, about loving and losing you. I am honoring the place you filled, and still fill, in my heart. It is sometimes challenging to write about your struggles, to revisit the ways I tried to help you but didn't always succeed, and to spend so much time sitting with my loss of you, but this writing also brings me comfort. It helps to keep your life and our relationship alive.

I was recently taking a yoga class taught by Caitlin, online in the living room, when I saw you in my mind's eye practicing your splits on the bare floor by the foot of the stairs, just feet from where I was practicing on my mat. You were plunked down on the wood floor, to help you slide lower. You were always so committed to doing whatever it took to be a better ballet dancer. You were such a hard worker, Colleen.

These reminders of you have been part of my life since you died, yet these days I experience these memories not just as bittersweet ponderings but also as inspiration as I write our story.

You lost so much along your way, Colleen, and I lost so many dreams I had for you. I am writing about those losses, while also honoring all that you brought to the lives of those around you.

As a child, you were funny, smart, and charming. People were drawn to you. You were a bright star, in many ways. Your humor was delightful. You could also be difficult, so headstrong, so all-knowing about what you needed and wanted. Primarily, though, you were smart and funny and kind.

You were a good sister to Caitlin, proud of her accomplishments, right to the end. She misses you, Colleen. Losing you has had a big impact on her life. Having had a sister and having one no more is something she talks about with me. She talks about when and how to share this part of herself with new friends. We spoke on the phone early this morning. She always does something special to honor you on your birthday, as well as on your death day. When she was living in New York City, she took ballet classes on your days. Now, living in Burlington, she finds other ways to honor you, the sister she loved and lost. We have been talking about our blooming lilies of the valley this year, mine here at home and hers in her yard up north. We will both pick some today, to honor that tradition the two of you shared, the games you two played with those flowers when you were young.

I loved you when you were a challenging baby, child, and teenager, Colleen. As a young child, you reminded me of myself when I was young, the best parts of my being young. As you grew older, I delighted in who you were becoming. I also worried about the struggles you were beginning to experience. Your teenaged years were challenging for both of us, but I continued to love you with all my heart--even when you became an adult who made choices that devastated me.

My life continues to be informed by my experience of both loving and losing you. You challenged me, and you changed me. Thank you, Colleen, for coming into my life. Thank you for loving me even when you couldn't say it. Thank you for being my daughter for as long as you were able.

3

Meeting Colleen

I HAD BEEN IN EARLY LABOR throughout the night, but my husband, Joe, and I chose to take some back roads to town on that glorious mid-May morning in rural Vermont. We marveled at the beauty of the bright, sunny, spring-green world on this day I would give birth to our first child. Crabapples were blooming in varying shades of pink and white; there were puffy white clouds in a blue sky. We were in no hurry to get to the hospital that morning because my labor seemed to be progressing quite slowly.

My pregnancy with Colleen had been uneventful, yet it was with some drama that she entered this world. When we arrived at the birth center, the obstetrician on call identified a complication and strongly recommended a Cesarean birth. I asked a few questions, weighed my options aloud, and took the time I needed to decide how we would proceed. Once I agreed to the surgery, I was asked to sign a consent form. Suddenly, nurses scurried around trying to get me out of my clothes and into a gown while I held a clipboard and pen. This surgery, I quickly realized, was being treated as an emergency. I was wheeled down the hall while Joe was told he could follow but would have to watch the birth through a window from the corridor. This was the protocol for a surgery involving general anesthesia. I could say that I wasn't awake as Colleen emerged into this world, but the truth is that I did hear her cry from deep within my otherwise unconscious state. That cry told me she was alive—all that I needed to know at that moment.

The birth center was overcrowded that day, so I spent some time alone in a recovery room. Colleen was a full two hours out of the womb when a bed was available to me, and I finally met her. She had spent those two hours with her father, who had held her and sung to her. I loved that Joe had had a chance to begin to bond with her before she and I met. Colleen was swaddled and calm when she was placed in my arms, and she was beautiful. No conehead for Colleen, as she had not traveled through the birth canal. She had a full head of black hair, bright blue eyes, and fair skin. A nurse told me that her eyes were not the blue that was typical of newborns; her eyes were already a deep blue that would not change. Colleen weighed a hefty nine pounds, four ounces. I joked, in those early days, that she looked ready for kindergarten. I liked that she was a good-sized newborn, as I had had no experience with babies that young. Colleen seemed substantial, not frail, and she had a very lusty cry.

Colleen was not a sleepy newborn. She was wakeful, and she was hungry, seemingly always, and she was very good at making her needs known. I was tired during those early days, from both the incision in my abdomen and the apparent insatiability of this baby of mine. Colleen took easily to breastfeeding and she seemed to want to do nothing but that. After one of Colleen's many sessions of draining each breast, I gazed at her in wonder. My wonder in that moment had nothing to do with the miracle of life. I wondered, instead, what she wanted from me. Too much, it seemed. She was ever present and ever persistent with her need, and I just wanted to rest.

I suppose most new mothers feel this way at some point, that their newborns want too much from them, but I also know that some women must wake their sleepy babies to feed them. As a newborn, Colleen slept only ten hours in any twenty-four-hour day, far fewer than I had been promised by books for expectant mothers. My sister-in-law, who gave birth to her first child three months after Colleen was born, struggled with having to wake her baby every few hours. He just wanted to sleep. I was incredulous. She said this was a problem. He was rarely awake, except when she was able to rouse him for feeding. It seemed that he never cried, although I imagine he sometimes did. As Oakley got a bit older and was awake more often, he seemed to just look around. He was not demanding in his need for attention. Mothering him looked so easy. He took hours-long morning and afternoon naps throughout his first year. But Cynthia, my sister-in-law, had never yearned for a baby, and I had longed for one all my life. So when Colleen turned out to be wakeful and colicky (she would cry hard for five hours every evening throughout our first four months together), I told myself I could do this. I had wanted this child. I was a thirty-five-year-old woman who had waited a long time to have a baby; I was mature; I had skills; I had resources; I could do this. This is what I told myself, and so it became true that I could parent this challenging baby who took half-hour naps as an infant and quit napping altogether at age two. I could parent her when she became a challenging child and teenager. And I could do it well. It was not easy. It was never easy. Not in the beginning and not in the end.

4

Spunky Colleen

THAT WAKEFUL BABY who cried hard and often, to communicate her needs, grew into an extremely verbal child. Colleen was talking in full sentences, and even using past tense in her story telling, before her second birthday. She was never quiet while riding in the car, always telling stories and asking questions and demanding responses until sometimes I felt like my head was spinning as I tried to keep up. Her chatter was put forth with a vocabulary that defied her age, yet she delivered it in a very chirpy, young voice. She was, after all, a toddler.

Colleen was still in diapers and in a highchair when my mother was visiting one Sunday morning and I was serving grapefruit as a first course to our breakfast. As soon as Colleen saw me approaching the table with fruit, she stood in her highchair and reached an arm towards me.

"Give me one!" she exclaimed.

"Can you say *please*, Colleen?" I answered. She paused, looked around, and then turned back to me.

"Pleak," she responded.

"Colleen, the word is *please*. You know how to say *please*." I was trying to be firm in my response, despite my growing amusement.

Colleen paused again, for a bit longer this time. We three adults had time to wonder how this might end. Would this strong-willed girl acquiesce?

"Ple," was Colleen's final effort to get what she wanted without giving in to what we wanted from her.

She was met with silence. By now, Joe, my mother, and I were working hard to keep from grinning. The three of us were seated at the table, each with a half grapefruit in front of us. Colleen's bowl sat near mine. Still standing in her chair and now with hands on hips, she glanced slowly from Joe, to Gloria, and then to me.

With her head slightly cocked to one side and a distinct air of growing weary of our game, Colleen said, "Just give it to me."

Colleen often colored outside the lines with her behavior. Not exactly defiant, she was clever and had some pretty good ideas about how to get away with things. Add to this her advanced language development, and who knew what she would say next. When Colleen was two and a half, I asked her one day not to grab things from the counter or the table without asking me first. I had safety in mind. For instance, there might be a knife on the kitchen counter. Her answer to me was, "I'm not *grabbing*, I'm *taking*." I wondered how common it was for a two-year-old to defend her behavior with semantics. I was pretty sure this was outside the norm.

Looking back now, I can see that when Colleen was as young as two, she and I were already laying the groundwork for a relationship based on respecting each other's differences. My desire to teach her how to navigate the social world was often met with her need to maintain her independence. Colleen valued our intimacy but, as she was busy forming a strong, healthy attachment to me, she also needed to regularly test the waters of her individuality. It was as though she needed to know if I could handle her having an opposing stance and still be there as her home base. Would I still love her if she parried my guidance or my closeness?

In the months leading up to Colleen's third birthday, she developed a bedtime routine of telling me that she liked me but didn't love me. I continued to tell her I loved her each night as I was putting her to bed. As her birthday was drawing close, it occurred to me that she might need some help moving away from this position; she had never been one to change her mind easily. I suggested to her one evening that perhaps when she turned three, she might love me. She seemed open to this idea. It seemed that we had an agreement, however tenuous. On the night of her third birthday, as I was tucking her into bed, Colleen said once again that she liked me but didn't love me. I reminded her that she was three now and told her I thought she had agreed to love me at this age.

"Not until after my party!" she exclaimed. Her birthday party was planned for the next day. And sure enough, that next evening at bedtime, she told me she loved me. Apparently, a deal was a deal. Colleen continued to tell me she loved me every night for about six weeks. Then, one evening, she said, "I don't love you, but I like you . . . because I'm pretending to be two."

It was often hard for us to hide our amusement at the things Colleen said when she wanted to do something her way. One evening when she was four, Joe and I were sitting at our dining room table sharing a meal with her. Colleen began to use her hands to eat something that is typically eaten with a fork, so I said, "Colleen, we don't eat with our hands." To this she responded, without even glancing our way, "You don't. I do." Joe and I looked at each other with incredulousness. As in the past, we tried to hide our mirthful expressions, not that Colleen was looking at us; she was continuing to enjoy her dinner, her way. It would have been hard to argue the position Colleen was taking. Here she was, once again, coming out with something that both surprised us and left us speechless. She usually used a fork. We had never been told of bad table manners at preschool or at either grandmothers' homes, so we silently agreed with one another to let this go. We felt it was important to pick our battles; we didn't want to try to control our daughter. She had a strong spirit and a mind of her own. Safety first, and not much else, mattered to us. We stuck with that.

5

I Need to Know!

ONE EVENING, as I was putting four-year-old Colleen to bed, I began to feel weary. It had been a long day of attending to Colleen's questions and other needs. I had answered numerous queries from her as I had guided her through her bedtime routine, and once she had crawled into her bed, I had answered a few more. Finally, I told her that we were done for the day.

"Tomorrow will be another day," I said, recognizing my mother speaking through me. "I will answer more questions tomorrow. I am going to turn your light out now." I tucked Colleen in, gave her a kiss, and headed down to the kitchen.

As I was attempting to unwind by emptying the dishwasher, I heard Colleen call from her bed, "Is five plus five ten?!" Wanting to hold the line on the limit I had set, I called back that I would answer that question the next day, reminding her that we were all done for today. "But I need to know!" she cried.

Colleen had been interested in numbers from a very young age. (I had overheard her counting some blocks she was playing with when she was just eighteen months old.) I answered four-year-old Colleen's question that evening, from the kitchen. How could I ignore such desperation? "Yes, five plus five is ten. Now go to sleep, Colleen."

The next day I asked a friend with a daughter the same age to tell me about their bedtime routine and any challenges it entailed. Apparently, there was not this same intense need for information at their house, and questions were never math related.

Colleen went on to excel in mathematics, earning very high rankings in state and national competitions throughout her childhood and early teen years. She helped her peers with their math homework during middle school and high school, offering her help in the dance school dressing room, over the phone, and through a peer tutoring program at school. She did this out of kindness, and then later in her adolescence she earned some income as a math tutor. On weekends, she tutored several students taking AP calculus. Colleen never charged what she could have; she mostly just wanted to share her gift and help others.

When she had graduated high school, Colleen taught a full semester of pre-calculus to a younger friend she knew through dance. This friend had a scheduling conflict, and the faculty of the high school math department agreed that Colleen could deliver the course as a tutor. Colleen was legendary at the high school, so there was no objection to her teaching pre-calculus. They knew Colleen was a math whiz. She had, after all, earned a near perfect score on the math portion of the SAT when she took it in the eighth grade, before she had set foot in an algebra class. As she took that test, she didn't know the answers to two questions, but she was able to clear that all up with her math teacher the following Monday morning. Colleen did earn a perfect score on the verbal part of the college entrance test, that day when she was thirteen, but she was more interested in mathematics. Writing had already become challenging for her, due to her extreme perfectionism, but math was pure joy. There was always a right answer in math, with none of that ambiguity that existed in writing an essay. As a senior in high school, Colleen earned the highest score possible on both levels of AP Calculus exams. Because the second level was not taught at the local school, she studied for it on her own, over a two-month period, using an old textbook given to her by a math teacher.

Years later, a few days after Colleen died, this friend she had tutored in pre-calc wrote to me to say that the morning of Colleen's death, she (Sophia) had nailed a particularly difficult college math exam. Sophia had left the test feeling good and thinking how proud Colleen would be when she wrote to her about this win. When she learned of Colleen's death, Sophia wrote to me instead, attributing her success in part to Colleen's attention and support of her when she was a teenager. Sophia has moved forward with math as a focus in her life, now in a PhD math program, and she and I have stayed in touch.

When Colleen was four, she needed to know if five plus five was ten. Since Colleen's passing, Sophia has needed me to know what a strong influence Colleen had on her. And I deeply appreciate knowing how profoundly Colleen touched lives beyond mine.

6

A Good Bewembory

WHEN COLLEEN WAS FOUR, I bought her a picture book written by Dr. Suess. *When the Grinch Stole Christmas* seemed like a good idea, with the holiday season approaching. I was certain Colleen would enjoy the rhyming lines, the plot of the story, and the illustrations. This book seemed right up her alley.

Young children enjoy hearing a story over and over, so Joe and I ended up reading *The Grinch* to Colleen a couple of times each over the following few days. As I was preparing dinner one evening, I overheard her reciting the story. It's not a short story, as picture books go, but Colleen was clearly reciting it word for word. I left my post in the kitchen and found her sitting on the floor of our living room with the book open in her lap, turning the pages to cue her recitation. I listened quietly while she finished the book.

"Will you read it again, Colleen?" I asked. "I wasn't here for the whole story."

"OK," she chirped.

"Is it OK with you if I turn the tape recorder on?" I asked. Colleen had enjoyed listening to herself singing and counting to 100 by 10s a few weeks earlier, so she readily agreed.

I recorded Colleen because I found her dramatic reading of

this tale so engaging. I thought it might be fun for her to listen to it when she was older. As a child she was already known for her sharp memory, which she called her bewembory in her cheerful little voice. Perhaps because she had such a large vocabulary at a young age, she spoke with quite a few amusing mispronunciations. She had memorized other picture books that had been read to her, but her recitation of *The Grinch* grabbed my attention in a different way. Not only did she recite this relatively long story verbatim, but she included dramatic flair in places where I knew I had not used that level of expression. Had Joe? Certainly, neither of us had spoken with a British accent, as she did in several places. Who knew where that had come from?

When Colleen was twenty years old, she, Joe, Caitlin, and I began a tradition of listening to her taped recitation of *The Grinch* on Christmas Eve. We all laughed at the particularly dramatic parts. A few years later, when Colleen moved in with a boyfriend, she borrowed that cassette tape and an old cassette player that we keep for this purpose. She wanted Chris to hear her as a four-year-old reciting this story with flair. Colleen was not always proud of her younger self's accomplishments, often judging them to be imperfect, but she understood how engaging and funny this recitation was. I am sure it helped that she hadn't made any errors.

Caitlin and Joe and I listened to this recording again on Christmas eve of 2017, just a month after Colleen's death. Our lives had been changed forever by Colleen's passing, but we weren't about to let that steal our holiday. We all laughed and cried as we listened to her amusing recitation. We felt fortunate to be able to listen to Colleen's four-year-old self in our early days of learning to live without her as an adult.

7

Intuitive Colleen

AROUND THE TIME COLLEEN TURNED THREE, Joe and I began to talk about having another child. Before this point in Colleen's life, I had been unable to imagine adding a second child to our family. Parenting Colleen, who was not quick to disengage in the evening and always rose at 5 A.M., felt like a full-time job. I also had a busy professional career, working as a psychotherapist as well as teaching graduate courses. Colleen had napped little as a baby and toddler, having quit napping at all long before the age of three. But when she turned three, the level of attention she demanded felt a bit more manageable somehow. Perhaps I had simply become acclimated to being her mother. And then there was my biological clock ticking away again. I was thirty-eight and I had always thought it would be nice to have two children. I also thought that Colleen, who was so often the center of attention, would be well-served by sharing the limelight with a sibling.

Joe and I were very careful to discuss this matter of a baby only in whispered voices when Colleen was asleep behind a closed door. Our luck in conception held, and we were soon expecting a baby. Joe and I told no one. Even when my father came to visit for a few days that summer and I was feeling tired and nauseous,

I did not breathe a word. We didn't want to risk this news making its way to Colleen's ears before I was safely into my second trimester of pregnancy. However, shortly after I had conceived, Colleen started talking about the baby who would be coming to live with us in our new house.

That summer, we broke ground on some land we had bought a few years earlier. Colleen knew it would be a while before we moved into our new house, which was not yet built, but she was quite certain that a baby would join us there. In fact, this baby I was carrying was due to be born the following spring, just a few months after we were to move. Colleen talked about her sibling being a girl. I said little in response to her daily comments about this baby, other than the occasional "wouldn't that be nice." Then, just as I was entering my fourth month of pregnancy, I miscarried. Joe and I were able to keep this event from Colleen. The morning after this loss, I was snuggled up on our couch reading to her.

"I don't think a baby is coming to live with us," Colleen said, sighing.

"Probably not soon, honey, but maybe someday," I said, a wave of sadness suddenly coming over me.

Colleen didn't say another word about a sibling for nearly a year.

That miscarriage happened in September, and exactly a month later my father died. Losing Austin was Colleen's first experience with human death and my first experience with losing a close family member. I thought it would be great for our small family to experience a birth, but that wouldn't come for another two years.

The summer after the September miscarriage, Colleen had started talking occasionally about wanting a baby sister again. I had not yet conceived another child. I was thirty-nine and thinking that perhaps my fertility was dropping off with age.

One morning, Colleen and I were sitting out on our front steps together.

"What if it were just the three of us?" I asked. "What if a baby didn't join our family?" I was working on feeling OK with this possibility, and I wanted to see how Colleen would respond.

"But who will I play with?" she asked plaintively.

Colleen still wanted a sibling, and I felt that Joe and I could do with another, most likely different, experience of parenting. I knew I would be happy either way, but Colleen seemed quite convinced that our family needed another child.

I became pregnant again the following spring, a couple months before Colleen turned five. We didn't tell her. I was forty years old, so we were planning to have an amniocentesis test. This wouldn't happen until I was fifteen weeks pregnant, and then it would be another week or so before we would know the results. We didn't know what decisions we would make if test results indicated any significant abnormalities. Because of these unknowns, waiting to inform Colleen of this pregnancy seemed prudent.

I was cleaning up the kitchen on a summer morning when the phone rang. Colleen was busy at the table, writing and drawing. The call was from the hospital where the genetic testing had been done. I was informed that my results were in, they would be sent to my obstetrician, and they showed no abnormalities. I hadn't been terribly concerned about the test results but still felt relieved to hear this news. Then, the woman on the phone said that she knew I had asked that the sex of our baby be withheld, but she wanted me to know that I could change my mind; she could tell me right then and there whether I was carrying a boy or a girl.

"Of course, I am curious," I answered, "but no, I'd like to wait on that." I was choosing my words carefully so as not to give Colleen any sign of what was being discussed. I hung up the phone and glanced casually towards her. She was watching me intently.

"What?" she asked. She had a very serious expression on her face.

I paused.

"Just tell me what's going on," she said. So I told her she was going to be a big sister.

"Finally," she responded, with a grin.

8

Big Sister Colleen

"WHAT IS SHE WEARING?" asked Colleen, sounding very sweet over the telephone. It was the morning after I had given birth to her long-awaited sibling, the girl Colleen had always predicted this baby would be.

"She is wrapped in a white blankie that has some pink and blue stripes, and she is wearing a little white hat to keep her head warm. Grandma Ellie is going to bring you over this morning to meet her." Colleen ended up visiting us in the birth center twice that day, which happened to be my forty-first birthday. My mother, Grandma Gloria, picked her up at Ellie's on her way to see us in the afternoon. Colleen got to hold her sister (sitting down, of course), and she asked if Caitlin might like her toys that were in the baby bed, when she got fussy—a red thermometer case and a green aspirator bulb. It was not until then that I truly understood just how little she knew about newborns.

Our first few hours at home, the next day, were challenging for all of us. Colleen was allowed to sit on the couch with Caitlin on her lap and Joe or me sitting nearby. Colleen did not like this arrangement. She thought she should be allowed to walk around the house carrying her newborn sister. When we explained why that wasn't safe and repeatedly set limits on what she was allowed to do with Caitlin, Colleen became quite indignant and loudly announced, "I want my Caitlin time!" She demanded that we leave the room, which we did one at a time to lessen her feeling of being hemmed in by the two of us, but of course we did not leave her alone with the baby. It was a long afternoon.

The following morning when Joe dropped Colleen off at school, he explained to her kindergarten teacher that she was likely to be tired. Caitlin had cried most of the night. I had alternated between nursing and pacing with the baby and Colleen had followed me around the house for hours saying in a voice that could have been soothing to Caitlin had she been able to hear it above the din of her own wails, "It's OK, Caitlin, it's OK." Colleen was nothing but well-meaning in her enthusiasm for and dedication to her new role as big sister.

We soon settled into a routine. Having another baby who cried for hours every evening was not as hard on Joe and me as it had been the first time around. This time we knew viscerally, not just because of what we had been told or read, that these colicky days would eventually come to an end. As far as Colleen was concerned, the timing of Caitlin's crying sessions was manageable. Caitlin typically revved up just as one of us was putting Colleen to bed, and Colleen slept through most of that wailing. Daytimes were blissful for me, despite my lack of sleep at night. I just couldn't believe the amount of love my heart held, with not one but two beautiful healthy young children. Caitlin didn't nap much but, as a second child, she had a bouncing, dancing, singing, chattering five-year-old sister to watch. Caitlin was less demanding of my attention because of this, but also because she has always had a less intense personality than Colleen had. Colleen, for her part, was remarkably good at sharing me with this baby who never slept more than thirty minutes at a stretch during the day.

"OK, I think she's down. We have a half an hour. What do you want to do?" I asked on a cold, snowy winter afternoon. Colleen and I were co-conspirators. The baby was down for a nap but wouldn't be for long.

"Let's play cards," Colleen responded.

"Good idea," I said. "Let's play crazy eights. It's a game we can stop at any moment."

"I love crazy eights. I'll get the cards, Mommy."

We settled onto the couch to play, both of us happy to have some uninterrupted time together. And, sure enough, at just about the half hour mark, we heard Caitlin beginning to wake upstairs.

"Looks like we're going to have company," said Colleen good-naturedly.

Caitlin was OUR baby—mine and Colleen's and Joe's. When it was just us three girls at home, she was Colleen's and mine. I did get to be alone with Caitlin some weekday mornings, with Colleen off in kindergarten. I remember the glorious quiet when Joe and bouncing, talkative Colleen finally got out the door and I could just sit in the rocking chair and nurse. Other days I took Caitlin to work with me. But on those afternoons when I was home with both girls, spending time with the two of them was never hard. If I was busy with some household chore and Caitlin became fussy, Colleen would jump in to read to her, to try to make her laugh, to do whatever it took to calm her. Colleen was enthralled with her sister and with her role as big sister. And this remained true for the rest of Colleen's life.

9

A Good Mother

IN THE FALL OF 1995, when Colleen was five years old and I was about seven months pregnant, I was in the kitchen on a Saturday morning when Colleen discovered that her chewable fluoride tablets, from a newly opened bottle, were not the color she expected.

"They're purple! They're not pink! They're supposed to be pink!" she objected, loudly.

"They're the same thing as all the other tablets you've chewed, honey. They're just a different color this time," I said. I was trying to be patient. I feared where this was headed.

"Noooo," she wailed. "You have to take them back! They're supposed to be PINK! I have to have the pink ones!"

"Taking them back won't work, Colleen. This is the only color they have at the pharmacy right now. The purple ones are the same as the pink ones. They are the same size, they will taste the same, and they will help you grow strong teeth in the same way."

"But I can't take these!" she cried, tears streaking her face. "They aren't pink! They have to be pink! You have to take them back."

"Colleen, I understand that you love pink. I know that. But there is nothing to be done about the color of these pills."

"I'm not taking them! I can't take them!" She was continuing to cry loudly. "Take them back and get the pink ones!"

"OK, I'm putting them away now. You can stop crying. We are not going to talk about the pills anymore today."

Colleen continued to cry loudly, but I went ahead with cleaning up the kitchen. I tried to distract her from her plight with suggestions of activities she loved to do, artwork for one. I stopped what I was doing to pull out some art supplies. When that didn't work, I pulled out some picture books, put them on the couch in the living room, and suggested she do some reading. I thought a change of scene (from one room to another) might help to shift her mood, but Colleen was unable to switch her attention from this pill tragedy to something else, anything else.

How long did Colleen carry on, with no signs of letting up? How long did she demand pink pills? Twenty minutes? Thirty? Could it have been that long? How does a mother measure time when her demanding child is carrying on relentlessly? I just wanted her to stop.

I was standing near the stove with a frying pan in my hand (I had made pancakes for breakfast) when I suddenly felt an incredible urge to hit her on the head. With the pan. *This is how child abuse happens,* I thought. *Apparently, even a parent graced with self-control can have sudden and dangerous fantasies of shutting up a child who is unremittingly carrying on over a trivial matter.* Fortunately, I had the wherewithal to walk out the door. I was, not for the first time, putting myself in time-out. My husband was in the yard doing some autumn clean up. To him I said, "Your daughter is in the house melting down over the color of her fluoride tablets. I am leaving so I don't kill her."

Joe looked at me knowingly, and with compassion. Not that I had ever fled the premises in the past (past removals of self from scenes such as these had involved hiding behind a locked bedroom door), but I didn't need to say much to explain to him why I needed to leave now.

I drove away. I had no wallet, but no errand that needed doing anyway, so I drove several miles over a tree-lined dirt road (sooth-ingly beautiful in October) to the home of my close friend, Sarah. As I pulled in, unannounced, I found Sarah in her yard with a friend of hers I had not yet met. Sarah looked at me quizzically as I emerged from my car, and I said, "I was pretty close to hitting her with a frying pan, so I came over here instead."

Sarah turned to her friend and said, "Ann is a really good mother." She said this in defense of me, before any doubt about my competence could form in her new friend's mind. My comment about the frying pan had been hyperbole, but this woman who had never met me had no way of knowing that. And, man, did Sarah's statement feel validating to me. It was just what I needed to hear. Yes, I was a good mother. I had NOT hit my child with a frying pan. I had only felt the urge; I would never harm my daughter. Fleeing the scene had been a good decision.

10

Grace Period

WHEN COLLEEN WAS SEVEN, she became more reasonable. She stopped carrying on about what color cup I put her juice in. She stopped insisting on wearing an outfit if it was in the laundry pile. I thought of my Catholic upbringing and the notion of age seven as the Age of Reason. In Catholicism, seven-year-old children become accountable for their actions; they go to Confession and receive Communion, because they are seen as capable of knowing the difference between right and wrong. Jean Piaget, an early and renowned developmental theorist, also marked age seven as a time of transition to logical thought. I thought about all of this as I witnessed a welcomed change in my daughter. When Colleen was seven, I did not describe her as easy to live with, but I did say she was easier to live with than previously. She would become much more challenging to parent when she was ten, the age at which she would begin to secretly restrict her eating. But before that, for a few years, we were in what I now look back on as a grace period.

At school, Colleen was well-liked by her teachers. Hard working, curious, and smart, she never presented problem behavior. Despite her slowly increasing obsessive-compulsive symptoms, Colleen held it together during the school day. Her newfound ability to be reasonable seemed to modulate her inclinations to correct and control people, a trait that could sometimes trip her up in social interactions.

Colleen's third-grade teacher was her favorite. After her second-grade year, I met with the school principal about my concern that she had not been adequately challenged that year. It seemed that she had spent quite a bit of time helping her peers learn what she already knew. When the principal suggested that we have her skip a grade, I objected. I did not feel she was ready socially to jump to fourth from second. He told me that, alternatively, he had a third-grade teacher in mind for Colleen, a new hire. Ms. Lewis was not new to teaching, just new to this school.

Ms. Lewis and Colleen quickly became enamored with each other. Ms. Lewis was tickled by Colleen's sense of humor and honored, no doubt, by Colleen's appreciation of hers. She also provided appropriate academic challenges for Colleen, which my girl loved.

Colleen sometimes felt frustrated by the behavior of her classmates. She was there to learn, after all, and she saw the antics of some children in the class as standing in her way. As much as Colleen adored Ms. Lewis that year, I think she would have liked to have been in charge. I was amused to overhear Colleen teaching a class in her bedroom one afternoon after school. Her door was ajar as I passed by in the hallway. Her classmates were all represented, by name, with stuffed animals. There was one exception. In place of a child named Colleen, there was a girl in the class named Julia, which in real life was Ms. Lewis's first name. Colleen was the teacher of the class. I would have loved to have been privy to which stuffed animal stood for each character in her game, particularly Julia. I imagine that teacher Colleen was an owl and Julia a bunny, as bunnies were Colleen's favorite animals. But this was a private game, a private working-out of the school day, so I continued downstairs without further eavesdropping.

Most weekdays I was at work and Colleen at dance class or piano lessons or in a grandmother's care after school, but on the one or two days each week I was home with my girls in the late afternoon that year, I overheard Colleen playing this game. My take was that reversing these two roles, in the privacy of her bedroom, helped Colleen to keep her opinions to herself during the day.

Colleen's fourth-grade teacher was also an experienced and excellent educator; however, she and Colleen had a different relationship than Colleen had with Ms. Lewis. Rather than fully honoring Colleen's uniqueness, this teacher often challenged Colleen to be more like the other girls in the class. For instance, she would assign her to play certain games at recess, games that Colleen had no interest in. I understood that this teacher was well-meaning in her attempts to get Colleen to socialize in a more typical way, but Colleen hated this interference and often complained of it to me. I don't believe she ever played four-square or tetherball, despite being told to, but not complying with a teacher's assignment created conflict for her. She wanted me to intervene and rescue her from these demands. This I refused to do. I explained to Colleen that teachers take different approaches in helping children and she wouldn't always have teachers she liked as much as Ms. Lewis. I knew it best to let these two work out a relationship without my interference. Colleen needed to find a way in the world, particularly when meeting up with people who had personality traits resembling her own, without me stepping in as her advocate. And who was I to say what suggestions might work with Colleen when coming from someone other than me?

Colleen's fourth-grade teacher was astute in her observation that Colleen might have obsessive-compulsive disorder. My response to this suggestion, which she seemed to be sharing with me in hopes that I would seek help for Colleen, was that I thought that Colleen might be headed towards such a diagnosis, perhaps as she entered adolescence, but I didn't intend to have her evaluated at that point, at age nine. Colleen was functioning well enough at school, she was easier to be with at home than she had been when she was younger, and there was no way that we would have her take medication when she was doing well enough without. Besides all this, I didn't think she met the criteria of a diagnosis yet. The issues that her teacher pointed to were consistent with Colleen's strong identity as a girl who wore only dresses and did not play sports. Neither Joe nor I saw a big problem with her asserting her identity in these ways. While we recognized that Colleen had some control issues and that she was spending a lot of time with me and Caitlin when she could have been choosing to spend more time with peers, we were not inclined to intervene with psychiatric help. We thought she was doing all right, despite her rigidity in some areas.

All of this was to change in Colleen's fifth-grade year.

"Colleen, making a sandwich is not an art project. C'mon, honey, you're going to make us all late getting out the door." Colleen was sitting on the kitchen counter, methodically spreading a small amount of peanut butter onto a piece of bread. She still had the jelly to do, on the other slice. She was very carefully getting into each corner, all the while making sure her layer of peanut butter was of a consistent thickness (or thinness, I realized months later). I was perfectly willing to make her sandwich while she gathered her things into her backpack, but she had decided at the start of her fifth-grade year that she wanted to make her own lunch each morning. She had also shifted from eating two slices of toast to just one for breakfast. At the time, I did not see these changes in her eating habits as early signs that she might be restricting her food intake. This idea never occurred to me, not even in a fleeting manner. She was only ten years old.

Later that fall, I noticed that Colleen's body was changing. She was a bit thinner, but I attributed this to the pre-pubescent changes girls' bodies go through. It wasn't until the winter holiday break from school that I noticed just how little she was eating and how thin she had become. I later understood that this situation had been developing throughout the fall and had escalated quite rapidly in December.

The four of us were sitting in a Chinese restaurant, during that week between Christmas and New Year's. We had ordered a few dishes to share. Colleen put three tiny piles of food on her plate, barely more than several bites' worth. When I asked her about this, she said she wasn't very hungry. We had been out of town all day, it had been a long time since lunch, but she insisted this was all she could eat. On the drive home, I began to consider the idea that Colleen was purposely controlling her food intake. Was she concerned about the appearance of her body? How could this be? She was ten years old. We had no television reception at home. We had no women's magazines at home. We had no internet access. There was no scale in our home. I had never made a single comment about my weight or body image in front of my girls . . . or anywhere else. I was happy with my body; how could my ten-year-old daughter be concerned about hers? How could she be thinking she needed to watch her weight? Where had this come from? How was this happening? Her thinking was no longer reasonable.

11

Colonial Colleen

DESPITE COLLEEN'S GROWING OBSESSIONS, including her secret concerns about her developing pubescent body, she was the same kind, smart, often funny person she had always been. As she rapidly lost weight that January, she became less light-hearted and more and more distracted. Still, I thought her many fine traits were still evident when she entered the hospital at the end of that month. Her personality beyond her mental illness seemed to be lost on some of the hospital staff, even as she gained weight and her depression lifted.

I, myself, often felt misunderstood and sometimes criticized when meeting with staff members. A social worker, for instance, asked me to stop visiting Colleen every evening. He and I were meeting in the hospital cafeteria. "She needs to separate from you," he said.

"She is ten years old," I responded. "She may be on an adolescent floor, but she is not sixteen. And she is in a psych hospital, not at summer camp."

Still, he maintained his stance, and I told Colleen I would comply to some extent; I would be skipping visits now and then, not often, but we could talk on the phone those evenings if she wanted to. It was not easy for her, at her age, to be on a psych unit with teenagers. (For instance, one boy on the unit repeatedly asked her if she would suck his dick. I was happy to hear, from her, that she had no idea what that meant. She didn't appreciate his tone, however.)

More challenging for her was complying with eating an ever-increasing number of calories per day within short meal-times. Her first morning on the unit, she had chosen to eat rather than be fed through a tube. But to be anorectic and required to eat 3000 calories a day, divided over three half-hour meals, was not easy. There was also the confusion that sometimes ensued among the staff who monitored meals. Would she or would she not be given a nutritional supplement to drink after a meal when the half hour was over and she still had food on her plate? This conversation occurred one evening between two staff members on the elevator, with my daughter, as they all returned to the unit. Colleen, the good girl who was trying so hard to comply, felt extremely anxious in this situation. She hated the uncertainty of whether she would have to swallow that bad-tasting drink. She hated feeling she had failed when she was working so hard to do the right thing. She experienced the threat of this drink as a punishment for not eating faster. She relayed all of this to me over the phone that evening. Fortunately, I had an ally at the hospital, an acquaintance of mine. David was the father of a girl who danced with Colleen. An energetic person with a great sense of humor, David was someone I had always enjoyed. He wasn't just fun; he was very competent and knew how to get things done. I knew I could reach David on the unit early in the morning, so I called him the next day and he had an immediate solution to Colleen's problem. Rather than talk to the staff involved, which was what I thought he might do, he proposed a much more helpful solution. He would see to it that Colleen was given denser foods so she could get those calories down within the time allowed. This would also help with the bigger issue of how hard it was to eat so much food. David was a godsend.

There was a young therapist I met with at the hospital, just once. I suppose this was somehow part of the treatment plan, that I meet with this woman. I was not impressed with her. She asked me what it was like to be a psychotherapist myself and to have a daughter with mental illness. Writing this now, her question does not seem outrageous, but at the time it infuriated me. What a ridiculous question to ask! Not only did this therapist break a fundamental rule in asking a question out of her own curiosity (rather than with therapeutic intent), but she also conveyed an air of judgment as she spoke to me, or at least that's what I felt. She was later moved into a non-clinical role at the hospital, and I hoped that would be a better fit for her.

Another social worker, an intern, asked me to tell her about my relationship with Colleen, particularly how we spent time together. This intern was not young, more middle-aged, perhaps the same age as I was or even a bit older. She was studying social work at a reputable college, but she was new. When I mentioned that Colleen and I had been doing embroidery, she was aghast. (Or was she simply surprised and a bit judgmental in her response? I experienced her reaction at the time as one of horror.)

"Why would you do embroidery with your obsessive-compulsive daughter?" she asked. "Don't you see how that will increase her tendency towards detail and perfectionism?"

"No, I don't see it that way. I do things with Colleen that she enjoys doing," I answered. "She is fascinated with colonial life-styles and customs. Doing embroidery did not cause and does not contribute to her mental illness. It is simply an activity that she is interested in, so I have taught it to her. Did I develop OCD because I learned to embroider from my mother? No, I did not." I don't think I said all of this. I did say at least some of it and thought later that I could have said the rest. Her attitude stuck in my craw and still does.

School-aged Colleen, age seven through eleven, was very interested in colonial America. She had an American Girl Doll, and accompanying books, representing that period, and she was very drawn to the customs, clothing, and recipes of colonial times. As mother and daughter in the kitchen, we made many colonial breakfasts and desserts (before she turned ten, of course, when she stopped eating sweet foods).

The strong sense of order and symmetry in colonial era households appealed to Colleen. For instance, when a colonial table was laid for a meal, serving dishes were placed in a balanced and symmetrical manner. Colleen loved setting our table in this way. The area of the human brain that appreciates symmetry is typically overly developed in the case of a person with OCD, so it made sense that she would feel at home and secure with colonial customs. Her commitment to wearing only dresses, her need for her environment to be orderly, her interest in embroidery, all of this fit in with the colonial culture that she wholeheartedly embraced.

I found it extremely tiresome to have to explain that Colleen gravitated towards certain activities because of her personality, which was of course impacted by her OCD brain; embroidery and ballet did not lead to her mental illness. I also hated being put in a position of defending myself as a mother. I wondered how much I was being judged for being thin. In American culture, anorexia in teenaged girls is often viewed as a problem that stems from the mother and/or popular culture. I know that these influences are sometimes very real, but I grew so tired of explaining to professionals that I did not own a scale, never talked about my weight, never dieted, and had no women's magazines or television reception in our home. (This was long before social media became a part of children's lives.) It was hard enough to have a young daughter struggling with this disease without mother-blame coming my way.

By the end of Colleen's four-week hospital stay, she was at a healthy weight. This accomplishment had been very challenging for her, emotionally. I admired her compliance and her ability to push past her ambivalence. She left the hospital with a diagnosis of obsessive-compulsive disorder, and she was sent home on medication to treat that disorder. Taking those daily pills lessened some of her symptoms. She reported feeling sad that she no longer cared about her previous pattern of taking her vitamins in a pattern, day by day. (These chewable pills came in various colors and animal shapes.) Lessening her need to control all aspects of her world was the goal, but the loss of some things she did that were harmless and brought her enjoyment was hard for her.

Part of Colleen's discharge plan was that I would line up a psychiatrist to follow her medication and a psychotherapist to meet with her weekly. I had been looking for a therapist for Colleen for two months. Just as she was ready for discharge, I finally found someone willing and able to work with her. I felt tremendously relieved by this.

Colleen would go on to work with Nancy for six years. I have often described Nancy as my partner in raising her. This is not to minimize Joe's role, but simply to recognize Nancy as a person in our court without whom I don't know how we could have managed those years. At times, life with Colleen felt terribly unmanageable, but at least there was Nancy to talk with, to plan with, to work with Colleen, and to assist me in finding inpatient help when it became needed again. Nancy was an extremely competent psychotherapist, who knew how to talk to adults just as well as how to talk to kids. She was empathic in her relationship with me, but she offered me so much more, always thinking about next steps not just in her work with Colleen but also in relation to how Joe and I could react to and support our daughter. As important as all of this was, when I now think of Nancy's role in our lives, what stands out is her appreciation for Colleen's unique personality, her recognition of Colleen's finest traits, her dedication to helping this girl who she clearly cared for deeply, and her sadness when we met after Colleen's early death.

12

These Dreams of You: From the Past

November 7, 2019
Dear Colleen,

Last night I dreamt of you and me. When you appear in my dreams, you are always happy and healthy. What was different last night was that it was only my second dream since your death where you and I have appeared together.

I first dreamt of the two of us in January of 2018, several weeks after you died. In that dream, you and I were skating. I felt comforted when I woke because we had been in sync as we skated, sharing an activity we had loved to do together when you were a girl. But I also felt sad, as we had gone around the rink only a couple of times when we had been called off the ice for it to be resurfaced. Our time together had been cut short. It was not difficult to interpret this dream. I wanted more time with you, Colleen. I know it was time for you to go, but I wanted more time with you.

Last night's dream was powerful. I was driving east on Elliot Street in Brattleboro, in the present, two years after your death. I slowed to a stop as I approached the crosswalk near Everyone's Books, to allow for a girl who was following her mother across the street. This girl seemed familiar to me, so I followed her with my gaze. As she reached the sidewalk and turned west, still following behind her mother and now moving alongside my car, she turned her head towards me. She was a beautiful girl, with long dark wavy hair hanging loose around her face, her eyes bright. And I realized she was you!

You smiled at me—a big, warm smile. You appeared carefree and happy. I realized that the woman walking ahead of you was my younger self, as you appeared to be in your early teens. But I barely glanced at my forty-something self; I was so enthralled with this glimpse of you. And then the vision was gone, in the dream, and I was left sitting alone in my car.

I woke from this dream, this morning, feeling pleased with having seen smiling, healthy you. This sense of peace was quickly followed by that all-too-familiar sense of loss. Still, I held onto this vision of you. Your life was not easy at that age but, in my dream, you seemed to be having a good day. Or was that smile you gave me simply meant for me in my present life? Was it a gift from you to me today?

Thank you, Colleen, for appearing in my dream and for smiling at me. I have no words for how much I miss you.

13

What Do I Know About a Mongoose?

"WHAT DO I KNOW ABOUT A MONGOOSE?" I asked. I was standing in the doorway of my boss's office the day after a particularly challenging evening at home. I told Diane this question would be the title of a chapter in the book I would someday write about raising Colleen. That memoir was to be about raising a smart, talented girl with obsessive-compulsive disorder and anorexia nervosa who eventually prevailed over her mental illnesses. My story of Colleen and me has turned out differently than I imagined back then, but the story of the mongoose remains relevant.

It was the spring of Colleen's fifth-grade year, a couple of months after her first hospitalization, when she was given a homework assignment of writing a few sentences about mongooses. Not a high-stakes homework assignment, just something she was to spend a short amount of time on. But for perfectionistic Colleen, this was a very big deal. She had to get this RIGHT.

We didn't have internet access at home back in 2001. We did have an enormous dictionary that showed a picture of a mongoose and offered a brief description. I thought that was an adequate resource, but it was not enough for Colleen. Her stress over learning more about mongooses and drawing a precise picture of one took over our evening. She spent hours alternatively working on and carrying on about this assignment, doing her best to pull us all into worrying about this as much as she was. Neither Joe nor I were concerned about the results of her homework assignment, but we were very concerned about Colleen.

Colleen's anxiety and resulting behavior that evening was exhausting, for all of us. Her younger sister, Caitlin, remained on the fringes of our conversations and Colleen's fretting and crying by staying in her room, but sound carries in a small open design log house, so there was no getting fully out of earshot of the drama that was unfolding. Unfortunately, what happened that evening was not an unusual occurrence in our home. Colleen had become an extremely fretful child when it came to her performance in any area. She was an excellent student, in all subjects, but nothing she did felt good enough to her. Nothing short of perfect was acceptable to Colleen, despite how often we tried to explain that there is no such thing as perfect in most areas of life. This she could not abide. She *had* to get it right, whatever it was. Clearly, the medication she was taking to treat her obsessive thoughts and compulsive behaviors was not helping to the degree that anyone had hoped it would be.

Many medications would be tried over the years that followed, but none of them ever helped in the way that medications often help people with mood or anxiety disorders or people with milder cases of OCD. Sometimes, Colleen would stop taking her medications because of undesired side effects. Sometimes, she wouldn't take her medications because they *did* help alleviate her symptoms somewhat, and she didn't like feeling out of control. Colleen sometimes fought her mental illness, and she sometimes owned it as who she was, much in the way she so strongly owned other aspects of her identity throughout her life.

When Colleen was four years old, she'd liked the color pink so much that she changed her name to Pink. She was known as Pink throughout her second year of preschool, and she signed all her artwork with that new name.

"Hi, Pink." A tall slender woman I did not recognize was walking towards us on Main Street when she spoke to my daughter.

"Who is that?" I asked Colleen, once we were out of earshot of the friendly woman.

"Oh, she was at school the other day," answered Colleen. Apparently, not only was Colleen now out in the world enough that she knew people I didn't know, but at least some of them knew her by a different name.

When Colleen arrived in kindergarten, at age five, her teacher asked her to sign her work with her "real" name. Colleen was not happy with this request, so she compromised by signing Pink Colleen throughout that year and the next. I thought this was a clever solution, and her teacher seemed satisfied with it.

By the time she was in the second grade, Colleen was no longer going by Pink or Pink Colleen. Sometime that year she began signing her name in full, not just her first and last names, but her middle initial as well. *Colleen E. McCloskey-Meyer* was her signature on all her schoolwork and artwork. Colleen liked being precise. When she was in the third grade, Ms. Lewis talked one day about a key on a map or document, and Colleen began adding one to the bottom of anything she signed, as in: *Key: E = Elizabeth.*

Not only did Colleen show her uniqueness with her name, but she also wore only pink clothes during the years she went by Pink. Her pink of choice was magenta; she was not the frilly sort. She also wore only dresses, from age six on. Nothing fancy in the dress category, but no pants for Pink Colleen. She typically wore a cardigan sweater over her dress. She was not at all fazed by the fact that none of her peers dressed the way she did. And once she swore off pants, she never made an exception throughout the rest of her life.

When Colleen was instructed to wear a pair of jeans for a performance with the middle school marching band in a parade in town, I bought a pair for her. The pants fit her perfectly and, to the rest of the family, she looked cute in them, but Colleen was so anxious about wearing jeans that her protestations stressed all of us. I felt my gut tighten as she cried from the top of the stairs that she could not do this. I tried to nudge her out of her very limited comfort zone by encouraging her to give it a try. I was trying to help this daughter of mine to navigate her world successfully. As parents, Joe and I wanted to honor her uniqueness while encouraging flexibility. I had never met such an inflexible person. Colleen's rigidity was becoming a bigger and bigger problem, for her and for the rest of us.

Colleen became louder, her voice shriller. Joe paced from room to room. Caitlin tried to stay busy, to keep a low profile doing something at the kitchen table. I was trying not to call the band teacher at his home to say that Colleen could not take part. Participation in this parade was a requirement of band membership. Had I telephoned sooner than I eventually did, Joe, Caitlin, my brother, Jim (visiting from the west coast at the time), and I would have been spared an hour or more of Colleen's carrying on in response to her internal angst about wearing pants.

After the call had been made and a sense of calm had settled over the household, I said to Jim, "What you witnessed this morning is an example of what goes on here all the time."

"Good god," he responded. I was after a bit of empathy, and I got it from him. I didn't need much, just a witness from time to time.

Identity, being unique, being good at all that she pursued, all of this became more and more important to Colleen as she grew up. Changing her name, dressing differently than her peers, choosing never to play sports ("no ball sports" was the way she put it) were all quite harmless when she was a child. Her refusal to play sports was not a problem in our eyes; she spent many hours a week dancing. But the level of stress she experienced when asked to wear a pair of pants for an hour (which I described to her as wearing a costume for a performance) was extreme. Her inability to comply with a brief change in her attire eliminated an opportunity for her to play her flute publicly, something she always enjoyed doing. The rigidity with which she defined herself was getting in her way of enjoying life to its fullest.

Eventually, Colleen's identity would become wrapped up in being the thinnest person alive, even if it killed her. She had become anorectic at the age of ten with—as I eventually learned from her—the goal of having a perfect ballet body. By the age of nineteen, she would be obsessed with being the thinnest person alive. If she eventually died in the process, at least she would have achieved her goal of having had the lowest body mass index of a living person.

14

Living with Mental Illness

DURING THE YEARS between Colleen's first hospitalization and her second, at age fourteen, our lives were filled with routine. Not just the usual routines of a family with children—getting them out the door to school, arranging for transportation to after-school activities, leaving work in time to retrieve them from wherever they were on a given day—but also the routines needed to make sure a child who doesn't want to eat her food does so anyway. There were weekly therapy sessions for Colleen, monthly meetings with a nutritionist, regular meetings with a psychiatrist who managed her medications, and Saturday morning weigh-ins at her pediatrician's office.

The weigh-in drill was that either Joe or I would leave the house early each Saturday morning with Colleen, before she had anything to eat, to drive her to her doctor's office five miles away. She would check in, use the bathroom, change into a light night-gown that was kept in a cupboard there for her, and get weighed by a nurse. Her weight was recorded. Then she would get dressed, be driven back home to eat breakfast, put her dance clothes on and get her hair into a perfect bun (not just a bun, but a perfect one), and then be driven five miles to her 10 A.M. dance class. The agreement (made by her treatment team of psychotherapist, medical doctor, nutritionist, and psychiatrist) was that she needed to keep a minimum weight, prescribed by her doctor, to be allowed to dance. Because she was so young and still growing, there was a new weight goal set up for her every three months. She needed to continue to gain weight on a regular basis so that she would grow. Studying ballet was contingent on her compliance. Ballet was of utmost importance to her in those years, so it made sense that we used it as our bargaining chip. The threat of losing this privilege also made sense as a somewhat natural consequence of being underweight.

Colleen hated putting weight on, even though she was getting taller, so she held out during each three-month period until the last week. Then she would adjust her eating habits to show the minimum gain needed at the scale. How did she do this so adeptly? She was a mathematician. She counted every calorie and ate exact amounts of food until it was time to increase those calories. Then, having met the new weight goal, she would hold herself at that precise weight for another three months. If she was slightly over the minimum weight required, she would cut back on her calories to be at that minimum the next week. She made this look easy, but I knew she was spending a lot of time scheming and managing the whole project. We still had no scale at home, so she relied on those Saturday weigh-ins to dictate her plan each week.

This regime of weigh-ins did nothing to treat her obsessive-compulsive symptoms; it was meant only to keep her physically healthy and growing. OCD was the disorder underlying her anorexia and needed to be treated as well. When Colleen was younger and I had suspected she might end up with an OCD diagnosis someday, it never occurred to me that this disorder might manifest as anorexia. While it is not at all unusual for people with anorexia to also have OCD (with perfectionism as the common denominator of the two disorders) most people with OCD do not become anorectic.

Joe and I did not always agree on how to respond to Colleen's behavior. I no longer remember the specifics of those disagreements, only that there was a time when we became so quickly polarized in our conversations that we took to emailing each other rather than talking. One morning I read an email from Joe that he had written in the middle of the night. Neither of us slept well, mainly due to our concerns about our daughter but also sometimes due to our discord over how to respond to her. The only major issue we have fought about throughout our long marriage has been how to deal with our starving daughter. Raising a child with mental illness can place a huge strain on a relationship. We did come through this with our marriage intact. I feel that our current bond has been positively influenced by our shared experience of losing this girl. Each of us loved her fiercely, and we each tried as hard as we could to help her, in our own ways.

Colleen continued to excel academically in middle school, but at a great cost to her happiness. She could still relax at times, particularly when spending time with her sister, but her need to achieve and to do so with perfection was a driving force behind her behavior so much of the time.

Towards the end of eighth grade, a meeting was called at school to address Colleen's transition to high school the following fall. In attendance were the middle school vice principal, the guidance counselor who would be assigned to her the following year, a special educator coordinator for the school district, Nancy, and me. Did Colleen already have a 504 Plan providing some accommodations at school due to her OCD diagnosis? I imagine she did; why else would the special ed person have been present? Or maybe that accommodation plan was put in place during high school, with this meeting initiating that. So many efforts were made to support her throughout her adolescence that the timeline is sometimes vague in my memory. What I do recall about that eighth-grade meeting was my realization that her challenges had become very evident at school and that the people in charge of providing support were taking her situation seriously. School personnel were concerned about how to help her transition successfully from middle school to high school, which would pose many new challenges.

While I was deeply appreciative of the school's attention to Colleen's situation, I was also grappling with my emotional reactions to all that was being said in that meeting. It was while sitting in that room that I first realized just how obvious her challenges had become to all the adults in her life. Her extreme obsessive and compulsive symptoms were affecting her ability to function at school, not just at home while doing homework. I had already known this, but not to the extent that became apparent in the vice principal's office that day. This realization added to my dread of what would come next for her, as she entered high school and faced the increased demands of that setting.

As it turned out, Colleen entered the ninth grade no longer able to sign her name. Her perfectionism had become so severe that she had moved from a painstaking practice of signing, with small perfect letters that looked like they had been typeset, to an inability to sign at all. This became clear on the evening of the first school day, when she needed to fill out some forms. She spent hours and much angst trying to do this perfectly. She struggled in her bedroom. She struggled in the dining room. She just couldn't feel satisfied with any of her efforts. I saw that we were now in bigger trouble than ever.

As September progressed and Colleen's struggles escalated, Nancy and I researched inpatient programs for Colleen. I had taken Colleen to Yale University's Child Study Center in August for a very extensive evaluation. The experts at Yale recommended an intensive outpatient treatment center focused on anxiety disorders, at the University of Philadelphia. This choice posed many logistical and financial challenges. Colleen and I would have to move to Philadelphia. I would have to take a leave from work, with no pay. We would have to rent a place to live. Caitlin and Joe would be six hours away. But I explored it, nonetheless. In the end, my contact at that program, in consultation with her team of clinicians, recommended that we explore inpatient treatment at Rogers's Memorial Hospital in Wisconsin.

Nancy spent a good amount of time on the phone with a representative of the Wisconsin program, one which used a cognitive-behavioral approach to treatment. This had been Nancy's approach as well, the approach that is most often effective with OCD. The team at Yale had also strongly recommended this approach. As it became increasingly clear that Colleen needed intensive treatment to function in school, in dance classes, anywhere in her life, I began to negotiate with our insurance provider to cover an upcoming hospital stay. This was a slow and laborious process, with payment being denied in the end. I had also explored cognitive behavioral treatment at a larger clinic in Houston, but our insurance was unwilling to foot the bill at either placement. By the time that unexpected determination was made, plans for Colleen's stay in Wisconsin were well underway. We decided to remortgage our house rather than cancel Colleen's treatment. She needed more help than outpatient treatment could provide. And I needed to get her out of town before the late November performance of *The Nutcracker*.

Our local dance school teamed up with a professional ballet company from New York each fall, to present this holiday favorite. Local dancers were used to fill the children's roles on stage. Every young female ballet dancer in town dreamed of dancing the lead child role, but only two got to do so each year, one at each of two local shows. Being on stage with professional dancers, pairing with a professional male dancer, and acting and dancing a lead role were all parts of this dream. Girls who were selected to dance this part typically did so for two years. There was a lot of rehearsal time (including trips to the professional company's studio two hours away), and it made sense to not have to train two new dancers each year. Colleen had danced the part a year earlier at age thirteen, and she had not grown too tall to dance the part again at fourteen; however, the owner of our local dance school told me there was no way she could put Colleen on stage that fall. I understood this; my daughter's perfectionism and anxiety levels were just too high. Rehearsals alone would be too stressful for her and those around her. This news that she would not dance the part of Clara was very hard for Colleen to take, and the only way I was able to get her to stop fighting about this was to tell her that she would be in Wisconsin by showtime. So I had to get her out of town by then. We arranged for her to go when it looked like insurance would pay but before it was a done deal. As hard a financial blow as that non-payment was, there was no way around her hospitalization. We owed our daughter the chance to be treated at the best program available, not at a group home in our state, as was proposed by our state insurance. I knew far too much about group homes for adolescents to think that Colleen would receive the level of treatment she needed for her symptoms.

I took two days off from work in early November to fly to Wisconsin with Colleen, get her admitted to the program, and fly home the next morning. The night before Colleen and I flew out, we drove to Connecticut to stay with my close friend Judi, who lived not far from the airport. Colleen knew Judi well, as she also taught at the graduate school and often stayed overnight at our house. When we got out of our car in her driveway, Judi came out to greet us and help us carry our things in; she would be taking us to the airport in her car the next morning. There seemed to be a lot of baggage, and I told Judi that Colleen had packed a lot of paper, piles of academic work, none of which would be needed in Wisconsin or probably ever again. Judi offered the recycling bin in her garage, and I responded, "No, you don't understand.

NOTHING gets recycled or thrown out." Judi smiled, knowingly. I glanced at Colleen, at whose expense my comment had been made, and I saw her grin. She knew I was making fun of her, and she found it at least mildly amusing. I was making a joke as a way of surviving her craziness and perhaps gaining some needed empathy from my friend, but Colleen was able to step outside herself in that moment and get the humor. She was often able to do this, despite all the times she was so derailed by her obsessive and compulsive symptoms.

We were met at the airport in Wisconsin by a driver who worked for the hospital, as it was an hour or so outside the city. The driver seemed kind, and he remained mostly quiet during our trip. Colleen became very worked up as we traveled, focusing on an imperfect grade she had received on a keyboarding test at school. She had tried to get that teacher to change her 99 to 100, as she was certain there had been an error in the grading process. Colleen could not abide by a grade less than 100 appearing on her mid-semester transcript. She was beyond distraught. She *needed* me to follow up on this for her. She *needed* that error to be fixed. I tried talking sense, as always. I was well-accustomed to this approach not working, but I felt it was my obligation, to her, to continue to try. I was not interested in contacting her keyboarding teacher, but she eventually wore me down. I agreed to call or write him when back in Vermont later in the week. Our driver remained quiet that day. I felt embarrassed, for a few moments. Then I told myself he sees the likes of this behavior often enough. But I wondered, is it typically this bad? Driving me back to the airport the following morning, the hospital driver asked how Colleen was doing. It was kind of him to inquire about her. He did so without judgment, and I remember him for that.

The admission process at the hospital was grueling. A young woman in that office refused to allow Colleen upstairs before signing a form. Colleen could not sign the form. This was why we were there; she couldn't sign her name. I tried to explain this to the woman who was blocking our way with this requirement. I spent at least an hour going back and forth between Colleen in the waiting room and the window to the admissions officer. Most of that time was spent talking with Colleen, trying to get her to put anything at all down on the form. She stood with a clipboard in one hand and a pen in the other. She tried. She fretted. She cried. She was extremely stressed. I became more and more stressed. I asked the admissions person if an X would suffice. She reluctantly agreed. Colleen remained stymied. She told me she needed a ruler. I asked for a ruler. I don't recall if a ruler was ever issued. What I most remember is that we had come this far, from Vermont to Wisconsin, it had been a challenging trip, and we were now stalled in Admissions. I don't know how long we were there, although I am certain it was well over an hour. It was long enough that someone from upstairs called down to see if we had arrived, as we were now much later than expected. We were escorted to the unit, without Colleen having signed anything. The staff we met with were extremely apologetic about what had happened in Admissions, reassuring us that that experience was not representative of what Colleen would experience during her stay, and encouraging me to file a complaint. I never did that. I had too much else on my plate over the coming weeks, even with Colleen no longer in our immediate care.

15

Forever Young

THE MORNING AFTER LEAVING Colleen at the hospital in Wisconsin, I woke in my hotel room to learn that the presidential election the day before had not gone the way I had hoped. When I had gone to bed, it had still been a close race, and I had been hopeful that our nation would not be facing four more years with a president who I (and most Americans) did not support. This is simply to say that I was already not in a good mood when Colleen called.

She was very upset, crying, talking about how she had already that morning been misunderstood and falsely accused of behavior she had not engaged in, and that I couldn't leave her there. She had used the restroom alone after breakfast, not knowing she was breaking a rule. Apparently, anyone with an eating disorder needed to be accompanied to the restroom within a certain amount of time following a meal. She had not known this and was now under suspicion of vomiting, something she never did. I asked her if she had explained herself, and she said she had tried but no one was listening to her. Being falsely accused of a behavior she judged to be bad was very upsetting to this girl who so strongly identified as being good. I asked her to find someone I could talk to and to put that staff member on the phone with me. I then tried to explain to that person that a mistake had been made. I was met with the party line about the rule. I said that of course they didn't know her yet, but I could tell them that vomiting was not something she did, and more importantly, being falsely accused was extremely upsetting to her. I could tell by the response I got that I was wasting my time. They didn't know me either; they did know that kids do a lot of things that their parents don't know about. Not that this hospital worker said this to me, but of course this would be her thinking. My concern was dismissed. It was clear to me that I would have to let them work all this out without my involvement. Letting go of advocating for Colleen was not going to be easy, just as it had not been easy during her first hospital stay four years earlier.

Sitting in a plane on an airport tarmac a couple of hours later, I felt extremely ambivalent about leaving my daughter behind. The plane began to taxi and, as it took off, I was scared. Was I doing the right thing? I was leaving my girl behind in a program that I really couldn't know enough about, no matter how closely both Nancy and I had vetted it. It was up to Colleen to sink or swim there. We had reached a point of near desperation and had decided this was worth a try, our best shot at getting her the help she needed. But would she be OK there? Would the treatment work?

Many hours later, driving north to Vermont from the airport in Hartford, it rained hard. I was playing a cassette tape I had made of some of my favorite songs when Bob Dylan began to sing "Forever Young." *May your heart always be joyful /May your song always be sung . . .* yes, this is what I had dreamed for my daughter—to be her best self, to prevail over this illness so her talents, and especially her kindness and eagerness to help others, could shine. This song had become my companion during my commute to work and home again that fall.

May you build a ladder to the stars/And climb on every rung . . . I was suddenly so overcome I had to pull off the highway. The tears that I had kept at bay for the last few days flowed freely as I sat and listened. Tractor trailers screamed by, shuddering my car. *May you grow up to be righteous/May you grow up to be true/ May you always know the truth/And see the light surrounding you/ May you always be courageous/Stand upright and be strong.* It was Colleen's goodness and inner strength that I so loved and so desperately hoped would prevail over her perfectionism. I was raising this child to become someone, not to succumb to the monster her mental illness was becoming. *May you have a strong foundation/ When the winds of changes shift.* If only Colleen could just find that strong center of herself and let it prevail over her challenges. I so desperately wanted her to grow up to be strong and true, to become the person who I felt she was meant to be. And so, it was no surprise to me years later that hearing this song sung again, by Joan Baez, just a couple of weeks after Colleen's death, brought me to my knees on the bathroom floor.

I don't know how long I sat slumped over the steering wheel on that November day in 2004, but when I pulled back on the highway the rain had let up. A few miles down the road, a call came in from the psychiatrist associated with the program in Wisconsin. He wanted to introduce himself, share his impressions of Colleen, and get some more information from me.

"Hello, this is Peter Lake."

"I almost missed your call. I'm in my car and have been listening to Bob Dylan, loudly," I said.

"Good choice," he said. "I love Dylan." *We are off to a good start*, I thought.

Peter would prove to be very likeable. He was sharp, caring, and very interested in my perspective on my daughter. I would continually appreciate the time he took, in future conversations, to update me on her treatment.

A few days after that first call, when Dr. Lake and I spoke again, he said to me, "We see kids with extreme cases of OCD from all over the county, but I have not seen a worse case of perfection-ism." I was silent for a moment. His comment was powerful, both validating my experience of raising this girl and, at the same time, causing me to feel scared about her future. For years already, I had grappled with fears that Colleen would not overcome her anorexia, that this illness would become a life-long struggle for her and that she could even die young. I allowed myself little time in this head space, choosing optimism as a coping mechanism. But those fears, of which I never spoke, lurked in my mind, most often when lying awake at night during particularly difficult times. Dr. Lake did not offer a prognosis during that phone call, and I knew better than to ask for one. Who knew how successful this treatment for her OCD might be? He wasn't suggesting that it would not be successful, only that it would take a lot of hard work. I appreciated his candor.

Colleen's progress was slow over the next ten weeks. The orig-inal plan was for her to stay just six weeks, flying home a week before Christmas on my 50th birthday. It was hard to make the decision for her to stay longer, when it was clear that more time was needed. Joe and I discussed this at length. Staying meant she would not be home for the holidays, and that was really hard for me. Sending her back and forth would not work. It would be impossible to get her to return to Wisconsin if she were to come home for a visit. And so she stayed through for another four weeks. In the end, the team in Wisconsin considered her treatment a failure.

I did not see the results of Colleen's treatment in such black and white terms, nor did Nancy. Some progress had been made. She came home able to sign her name and hand in some school assignments. Essays were still way too challenging for her to sub-mit. She wrote well, but with there being no such thing as perfect writing, she couldn't imagine submitting anything. She continued to excel in math, which was all neat and tidy and made so much sense to her very logical mind. Unfortunately, she came to view all aspects of life through the lens of mathematics, and that often tripped her up. For instance, Colleen would never learn to drive a car, as she couldn't imagine being able to figure out exactly how far to move the steering wheel to make a turn. Without a mathematical formula, she would be stymied.

Colleen came home from Wisconsin on a new medication regime, which would be followed by her local psychiatrist. She saw Nancy three or four afternoons a week when she first returned to Vermont. The stage had been set for continued hard work using cognitive behavioral therapy methods. Colleen was able to engage in that work more fully than before her hospital stay in the mid-west. In that way, we saw her treatment there as helpful. We resumed the Saturday morning weigh-in drill, and she continued to dance. She resumed meeting with the nutritionist she had been seeing since shortly after her first hospitalization. Colleen made it through high school without another hospitalization.

16

These Dreams of You: Christmas Gift

December 26, 2021
Dear Colleen,

Christmas Day was an icy one this year, so our plan to host a dinner for some of the extended family was curtailed. Instead, Joe and Caitlin and I spent a quiet day together at home. Caitlin and I dressed for dinner, as though we were to have company. I was cooking the holiday meal that we had planned, so why not dress for it? After dinner, the three of us listened to the tape of you reading How The Grinch Stole Christmas. *Caitlin and I laughed; Joe cried. (Our loss of you strikes each of us in different ways at different moments.) A while later I went upstairs to change into something more comfortable. Caitlin and I were going to hang out and listen to music, something we often do evenings when we are together.*

I keep the clothes that I seldom wear in the closet of our guest room, the room that used to be yours. (I try to call it the guest room now; more often I still call it your room.) I went in to hang up my red velvety turtleneck (you know the one), but when I entered the room, I was suddenly aware of your presence. The room seemed to be filled with you. Not four-year-old you, who had recited The Grinch, *but an older you. A smiling, delightful older Colleen, perhaps late school-aged, perhaps early adolescent. I had not been thinking of you as I entered the room, but there you were, without warning, and I was both surprised and delighted by this. Not exactly a vision but more than a memory, your presence was strong and clear.*

Wanting to hold onto that moment, I stood at the foot of your bed (covered with that beautiful rose red, green, and white flowered quilt that you made in middle school), and I closed my eyes. When I opened them, my eyes landed on the moons and stars and planets still attached to the ceiling above where you slept. I had forgotten about those stickers, the ones that look slightly yellow by day or when a light is on, but then look so bright in a dark room after the switch has been flicked off. I was pleased that you had never taken them down. I soaked in those moments with you, hung up my shirt, and then floated out of the room feeling like I had been given a very special Christmas gift. As I passed through the doorway, I turned off the light and looked back at the glowing stars. Yes, they still work; they still hold light in the darkness.

After finishing a few tasks upstairs, I paused in the hallway and wondered what might happen if I were to go back into your room. Would you still be there? I slowly opened the door, entered quietly, and found just a spare room. Just a place where the Christmas wrappings lay strewn on the bed and my out of season clothes lay in a chest of drawers, a room where my sewing machine is set up on a table and where the occasional guest sleeps. I suppose that magical moments, like dreams, just happen when they happen, not when we go looking for them.

Back downstairs, I told Caitlin what I had experienced. She nodded in a very interested and thoughtful way. Caitlin is my partner in remembering you.

Thank you, Colleen, for coming around in this way, now and then. Your presence is always a welcomed gift.

17

Push-Pull

THROUGHOUT COLLEEN'S HIGH SCHOOL YEARS, she often needed me to advocate for her. I always tried to let her work things out with her teachers, case manager, and dance instructors without my interference. Sometimes I needed to step in. While educators and staff at the high school were well used to working with students with special needs, my daughter's needs were unique.

Due to her high intelligence, it was often difficult for teachers to understand how it was that Colleen could not hand in written assignments. She also needed more time on assignments because of her compulsion to check and re-check her work. And then there was the trouble with the AP Calculus teacher who became very upset with Colleen when she pointed out an error that the teacher had made.

Perhaps this math teacher had marked something wrong in Colleen's work when it was in fact correct. Or, perhaps, Colleen pointed to an error in her teaching in class. Whichever it was, Colleen tried to explain what was incorrect, but her teacher was not interested in being corrected and was not happy that Colleen did not quickly drop this matter. I know how persistent Colleen could be. A meeting was called, which Colleen and her case manager and I attended along with the calculus teacher. As in other meetings at the school, I tried to say little. I knew that Colleen needed me there as an ally, rather than to speak on her behalf, but she did tend to want me to rescue her from difficult situations. When she turned to me, after being asked a question, I reminded her that she could speak for herself. The math teacher, a middle-aged woman dressed as though she were older, was inflexible on the matter of having been corrected by Colleen in class. Despite Colleen speaking up in a respectful way in this meeting of adults, her teacher would not budge. She wanted Colleen to understand that she was not to challenge her authority, that she was to defer to her in class. Although the situation was not resolved to Colleen's satisfaction, my presence in the meeting had served to encourage Colleen to defend herself.

Our relationship outside of me being her ally was often marked by her very strong need to distance herself from me. She typically did this by criticizing my behavior, attempting to control me, and claiming extreme embarrassment of me. She could be quite nasty. I knew this separation behavior was typical of young teenage girls in relation to their mothers. But Colleen did not lighten up at age fourteen or fifteen; she kept going. Sometimes it all struck me as so ridiculous that I would laugh.

There was the time I ducked behind an open refrigerator door so she wouldn't see me laughing, but she knew what I was doing, and this added to her fury. Caitlin was often a witness to this. She found Colleen's attempts to restrict my behavior absurd. If Caitlin laughed along with me, we were both in trouble with Colleen, who of course wanted her sister to be her ally, not to side with me. Caitlin tried to stay out of the fray. Colleen saved most of her wrath for me. She hated it when I danced in the driver's seat of the car. (Caitlin enjoyed my enthusiasm for music.) Dancing in the kitchen was also verboten. Still, I did these things. Her constant scrutiny was tiresome, but I wasn't about to tiptoe around.

To this day, when I dance in my home, I am aware of a sense of freedom that I didn't feel in the years of Colleen's regime. I can dance with abandon in my living room now, no longer hearing her objections and judgment over my shoulder. As annoying and sometimes confining as her loud and angry objections were in the moment, I did understand that not only did she have control issues because of her OCD, but it was also extremely challenging to be a teenager so dependent on her mother for advocacy. Her developmental task was to pull away, but she often needed my help. I was glad to have a background in psychology to help me understand this daughter of mine.

There were times when Colleen carried on about something that had nothing to do with me, yet she wanted me to somehow do something about her plight. Sometimes I lost my patience with her. I don't know what the specifics were one evening when Joe was not home, and I decided I needed to leave the house to get away from Colleen. As I was putting the car into reverse, Caitlin (age nine, perhaps) came flying out the door and jumped into the back seat. "I'm coming!" she yelled. Caitlin did not want to be left behind with her anxious, demanding, shrieking sister. We didn't travel far, but we were gone long enough for Colleen to settle a bit and be more reasonable when we returned. This was not unlike when she was four and I couldn't get her to sit in time-out. I would put myself in time-out, instead. I would go into my bedroom and lock my door. Physical separation was the only thing that worked when she was whipped up and unable to stop demanding whatever she was after. When it didn't work to calm her, at least I was able to get away from a frustrating situation that I was having no impact upon. When she was four, sequestering myself in my bedroom worked for me a few times, before the lock was broken by her wailing against the door as I tried to secure it. Joe and I would have had to rehang that door to get the lock to line up and work again, something we never got to. We were quite busy with two careers and two children, one of whom was becoming more challenging to parent each year.

I don't know what she said or how many times she said it, when I lost my patience with adolescent Colleen one evening in the living room. I recall some details about the physical scene—where she stood, where I sat—but nothing of what was so upsetting to her or what she was demanding of me when I realized that I needed to leave the room. I needed to get away from her. Colleen kept at me as I moved past her with a glass of water in my hand. I was as surprised as she when I lost control of that glass and its contents landed in her face. Joe and Caitlin (who were in the room as well) were surprised as well. I was not proud of this moment. It was the only time I could recall losing control of my behavior in the face of the challenges she threw my way. Her face was wet, she was shocked, and Joe said to her, "You had that coming." I quickly jumped in to apologize to her. She deserved an apology, not criticism from another parent in that moment, but I also felt supported by his reaction. I was feeling some guilt about losing my patience with her, so I appreciated not feeling judged by my partner. Just as Joe and I had taken turns pacing the house at night with colicky babies, we did a good job stepping in to support each other during Colleen's teenage years.

18

Lost Talents

COLLEEN'S ADOLESCENT YEARS were wrought with challenge for me, but no matter how difficult it was to raise a child who had both obsessive-compulsive disorder and anorexia, living with these disorders was infinitely more difficult for her. Holding this in mind helped me to maintain compassion during times when I felt angry or impatient with her.

When I was a young child, like so many other children, I made wishes upon stars on clear nights.

Star light, star bright,
First star I see tonight,
I wish I may, I wish I might,
Have the wish I wish tonight.

I taught this poem to my daughters when they were young. Living in a rural setting, without the interference of artificial light, cold clear winter skies offered many opportunities to look up in awe. The girls liked reciting the poem and making secret wishes. I also loved gazing at the night sky, but I rarely made a wish. I tended more towards scientific thinking as an adult, rather than what I thought of as magical thinking.

In the months following Colleen's first hospitalization for anorexia, I found myself wishing upon stars again. It was obvious to me that, despite my dedication to Colleen's recovery, there was much that was out of my control. My wish, for the next fourteen years, was always to be the same. From the winter of 2001 until the spring of 2015, I wished that Colleen would recover.

My wish did not come true, but it was not until two and half years before her death that I realized with certainty that it would not. For fourteen years, I continued to hope for her, despite witnessing loss after loss in her life.

Colleen had many talents growing up. She played the piano and the flute beautifully. She was accomplished in ballet, and she was an excellent student academically. Between her giftedness and her hard work, she was successful at whatever she took up.

Colleen wrote lyrical poetry in elementary school. She framed for me a poem she wrote in the third grade, with dried flowers dancing around the edges.

A flower, yellow as sun,
All alone upon a hill.
Rain splashes down on her.
The shower now done,
The flower sits still,
Her wet petals all in a blur.

Colleen was an early and impressive artist. Her first representational drawing was done when she was just barely two years old. We were sitting outside in the sun at her child-sized picnic table one spring day when she drew two circles and connected them with a line. "This is sunglasses," she said. I knew this was unusual for a child her age. She went on to make beautiful art both at home and at school as she grew. She was a realist, so she mostly made realistic drawings, with a brilliant use of color.

By the time Colleen was in middle school, she was no longer making art or writing anything creative. By the time she entered high school, she wasn't writing anything at all. Extreme perfectionism, a severe symptom of her obsessive-compulsive disorder, stole all of that from her. She still played her flute and excelled in math. And she danced. Dance was the last of her artistic talents to go.

Carrie was Colleen's favorite dance teacher. They shared a deep appreciation and knowledge of everything ballet. Carrie taught locally at the dance school where Colleen grew up. Colleen had many other influences on her ballet technique, mostly from teachers in summer programs she attended, but Carrie and Colleen formed an unusually strong bond. As a teacher, Carrie had rarely, if ever, fielded as many questions as she did from this serious student of hers. Colleen was beyond inquisitive; she was full of information about ballet and always looking for more. She was very focused on ballet technique, much of which was gleaned from the hours upon hours of classical ballets she viewed on VHS tapes, both her own and Carrie's. Colleen's commitment to perfect technique would eventually hurt her flow as a dancer, but even then, she and Carrie had many conversations both in and out of class about how ballet was to be performed.

During her junior year of high school, Colleen's questions about technique in dance classes became incessant. Carrie taught Colleen both in classes at the dance school and in classes during the school day through the career center. By spring, Colleen became an obstructionist in Carrie's classes, unwilling to budge from her need to get every one of her questions answered on the spot. Carrie was unable to control the flow of a class because of the amount of minutia that Colleen wanted to have addressed. She sometimes asked reasonable questions about why something was to be done the way Carrie taught it, but she also asked questions from a place of wanting to show off what she understood. And her need to get ballet technique perfectly correct led to far too many questions. Carrie drew up a contract for Colleen, which addressed how many times she would be allowed to speak per class; limited her ability to stand wherever she wanted, to always see herself in the mirror (a behavior that often got in the way of at least one other dancer); and disallowed eye rolls (something she had been falling into when questions asked by others seemed silly to her). Adhering to this contract made it possible for Colleen to complete the school year in the dance program classes, but it also prompted a meeting at the high school career center late that spring. Around the conference table sat the two dance teachers who managed and did most of the teaching in the dance program, the head of the career center, the career center counselor, Colleen, and me. Carrie, as an adjunct in that program, was not present. I did not know the full purpose of the meeting before arriving, nor did Colleen.

The meeting had been called to explain to Colleen that she would not be allowed to study dance through the career center the following school year. This was an enormous blow for her. The career center dance program bussed dancers to the local dance school for a full block of classes, five days a week. The dancers ate their lunches on the bus. Colleen had been involved in this program, in addition to all of her after school and weekend classes, since the fall of her first year in high school. Dance was her life, so to speak. What became clear at this meeting was that, while she would still be dancing outside of the school day, for the first time in her high school years, she would be dancing less rather than more and needing to find a way to navigate lunchtimes at the high school.

"Wait, what? What are you saying?" This was hard for Colleen to take in. She turned to me with a frantic expression on her face. I was also surprised, but I did not respond. Most of the adults in the room appeared to have somewhat unkind expressions on their faces, most likely because they needed to hold firm. They knew who they were dealing with. They knew this would not be a decision easily accepted by Colleen.

Colleen did not quit dancing after this intervention. She went away to dance for four or five weeks that summer at the prestigious ballet school in Philadelphia she had been attending for several years. She danced several days a week in the fall, with me driving her to a dance school in New Hampshire on Monday evenings so she could fit in a class with a different teacher. But when spring registration rolled around that winter, she decided not to dance anywhere. It had all become too stressful for her, as she aimed for perfection and faced her limitations as a ballet dancer. Her need to get it all right had gotten in the way of her flow. She often wanted dances to be slowed down so she could get through a checklist in her head of technique with every move. In rehearsals for performances, she was often behind the music. My untrained eye did not catch this, but Carrie repeatedly pointed this out during that spring of Colleen's junior year. Her OCD had ruined dance for her. While this was a huge loss for Colleen, and a very sad one for me to witness, I also felt some relief. Her need to get it all perfectly correct had increasingly been interrupting her enjoyment of the process, had led to her agonizing outside of classes, and had increased both of our stress levels.

For the rest of Colleen's life, she would continue to study ballet as an audience member, traveling to New York City solo when she was a teenager to attend American Ballet Theater performances. She began to take her sister along when she was about twenty and Caitlin fifteen. Later, when Caitlin was studying dance in college on Long Island, they occasionally met in the city to attend performances together.

Colleen continued to mentor other dance students at the local dance school. She worked with choreographers, as a ballet assistant, when they were holding rehearsals for the annual dance school performances. Colleen was a good assistant, as she remembered with exactness any piece she had danced or had watched performed, on video or in person. She did have that amazing "bewembory." This volunteer work was really a continuation of the mentoring she had offered her peers throughout high school. There was a long stretch of time during her adolescence when she insisted on arriving an hour early for her Saturday morning class, to help dancers who took more time to learn choreography. They would arrange to work with Colleen before Saturday class, to learn pieces for upcoming performances. They needed a bit more time, and Colleen was always eager to help.

A few weeks after Colleen's death, a close friend of Caitlin's, who was also a friend of Colleen's, wrote this tribute on Facebook:

I've stayed under the radar for a couple weeks because of being sick/still processing, but I wanted to write something about Colleen McCloskey-Meyer.

I met Colleen when I was eleven years old (besides having earlier been a finale clown in the Nutcracker when Colleen was Clara). I was the youngest student in Carrie Towle's Saturday class, and we stood at the center barre together with Sophia Marx. Anyone who knew me then could attest to the fact that I was a mess. I'm not necessarily referring to the fact that my dad had died that year; I also mean that my technique was hilariously bad, and I was in a class full of intimidatingly good dancers without knowing what a waltz turn was.

But Colleen was good. Like, really good. And she is one of the few people who I think would've wanted to be remembered as much for her classical technique as for her kindness. I am part of a lucky few who got to see her dance, and I am even luckier to have known her. Colleen was a fighter, a good listener, and incredibly honest. I was lucky to grow up in her family through becoming best friends with Caitlin McCloskey-Meyer. Colleen was one of the first people I met who shared (and definitely surpassed) my intense love for ballet. When Caitlin and I had slumber parties at her house, Colleen and

I would spend hours watching Corsaire, Center Stage, *and even the* Balanchine Essays *on VHS. She would time my balance in attitude in Ann McCloskey's kitchen to see how it compared (unfavorably) to Alina Cojacaru's.*

Colleen paid attention to me at a time of my life when I felt invisible in many ways. She shaped the way I see ballet. I owe so much of any technique I have today to her help. She spent countless hours in the studio coaching me over the years. If she were here to comment, she'd agree that helping my sad, bent-kneed, floppy-armed self from age twelve onward was an act of self-sacrificial charity.

We never got a picture together, as far as I know, so I thought I would post this photo of the Yuka Kodama Ballet Group show from last year instead. I'm smiling here because I've successfully done a set of Italian fouettés, a step which has been my enemy for about ten years. When I began rehearsals for the show last spring, I predictably texted Colleen for help. Across the ocean, she offered me tips for my variation, historical contexts of the ballets we were performing, and tips on the fouettés (a word which she incidentally taught me to spell at age twelve). After so many years, she was there for me.

This past year, my Oxford tutor said to me, "My religion is kindness. Not being 'nice,' but real kindness." This is how I think of Colleen now. She was an incredibly loyal and giving person, and she understood that honesty is a form of love. I could always count on her to make great jokes and to listen attentively. She was odd, she was hilarious, she was a genius, and she was kind. She cared so much for ballet and others. She was a big part of the BSD community and one of my closest and oldest friends. I will miss her a lot, but I won't forget her friendship and her great and unwavering love for ballet. Over my lifetime I have often felt "too much" for people: too energetic or enthusiastic or something. I never, ever felt "too much" for Colleen. I'm really grateful for that.

—Lena Serkin Mazel, December 2017

Colleen's behavior in classes when she was sixteen caused her peers to shift, for a while, from being tolerant of her to being annoyed with her. When Colleen's behavior obstructed the flow of classes, her peers became impatient. Once Colleen stopped dancing, losing something she had loved to do for so long, she found a way to bring her kindness to the fore and help others with her knowledge and love of the art form. After Colleen's death in 2017, an annual memorial class was established, to raise funds for a dance scholarship in Colleen's name and to bring alumni of the dance school together. Carrie teaches the class each year and students either attend in person or online from around the country. I have been struck with the kindness with which her peers remember her. Carrie presents difficult combinations in class, as Colleen would have liked. She tells stories of Colleen in relation to the combinations she teaches. The dancers have fun dancing, enjoy seeing each other, and remember Colleen fondly.

19

A Near Miss

IN MAY OF 2008, as Colleen was approaching her eighteenth birthday, she began losing weight again. Having stopped dancing a few months earlier, we could no longer hold that privilege over her behavior. I could see that she was losing fast, over a matter of just days. She had, for many years, held herself at the minimum weight allowed by her doctor. Colleen was only four feet ten inches tall. She had, most likely, stunted her growth by holding her weight back for so many years, something she began to do before puberty. She was required to weigh no less than ninety pounds in her late adolescence. So, it was clear when she started to lose. A few pounds in either direction on a person her size was noticeable. Never having been one to do something half-heartedly, she was an expert at fast weight loss.

Colleen was not in therapy at that point in her adolescence. When she was sixteen, she and Nancy had decided together that it was time to take a break. Colleen wasn't doing the work required of her in therapy anymore and Nancy felt it would be better to stop meeting, with an open invitation to Colleen to resume when she felt more ready to re-engage in the hard work of challenging her obsessive-compulsive symptoms. I agreed with this thinking. But now it was hard to watch Colleen decompensating without the safety nets of psychotherapy and dance.

She was in the kitchen getting ready for school one morning when I made a point of joining her at the utensil drawer. I needed to get close enough to smell her breath. "You have that smell, Colleen. You're in ketosis," I said, as matter-of-factly as I could manage. I was trying hard to keep emotion out of my voice. I was not looking for a fight; I just wanted her to know that I was noticing what she was doing. She would know what my noticing meant.

"Leave me alone," she shot back. "I know what I'm doing."

"I know what you're doing too. And I'm not going to put up with it."

"Just get out of my way. You're making me late for school," she snarled.

Joe and I exchanged glances. We had been here before. We hated this place. But we were a team, and we would talk later.

I went to work but spent a good part of the day on the telephone. I talked with Joe, and I got an appointment for Colleen with her psychiatrist, who she still saw monthly to manage her medications. I arranged an appointment with her pediatrician. It's amazing how easy it is to get last minute appointments when the patient is a repeat offender with anorexia. Both the psychiatrist's and the pediatrician's offices were within easy walking distance of the high school. Her appointments that day were scheduled back-to-back directly after school got out, so I texted the appointment times to Colleen and told her to be there.

I was not surprised when she didn't show up for the first appointment with her psychiatrist. She was quite ambivalent about her relationship with this man. Sometimes she liked him, but sometimes she didn't. I knew that she wasn't going to want to hear what he had to say that day. But Stu and I made good use of the half hour without Colleen. After hearing my report of the latest developments, he called our local psychiatric hospital and arranged for her to be admitted at any point over the weekend, with a simple phone call ahead from me. It was a Friday and Colleen was to turn eighteen on Monday. I had figured out what she was up to. She had most likely been planning for a very long time that she would lose weight when she was eighteen—legally too old for us, as her parents, to do much of anything about getting her admitted to a hospital. At least, that was how she thought. She was right, to an extent. It would be much harder to get her into a hospital against her will once she was of age.

Colleen did turn up at her doctor's office a half hour later. I was pleasantly surprised by this. The two of us had a long conversation with her doctor. It was then that I told her my plan for the weekend, which I had hatched with Stu's help. She was to start eating, under my supervision, or she was going back to the Brattleboro Retreat, the hospital she had spent a month in when she was ten. She argued, but she could see that she was outnumbered. This was when she realized she had taken her weight down too quickly. Defeated, she eventually agreed to start eating normally again, over the weekend, with me overseeing.

When we got into my car, she told me about having been invited to a sleepover with two other girls that evening. One of her oldest friends, a girl she had met in pre-school when they were just three, had asked her to join in for an evening of watching movies at her house. She and Sarah had not spent time together, outside of school, in years. The details of how this invitation came about elude me now; I recall just that it was Colleen's understanding that these two girls wanted to talk with her about her recent weight loss and encourage her to gain and stay healthy. I knew these girls, as well as Sarah's family, so I agreed that Colleen could spend the night encouraging her to eat while there. I went in and spoke with Sarah's mother. I let everyone know I would be back in the morning. I had already told Colleen I would retrieve her early so she could come home for breakfast; I was skeptical that she would resume eating in front of others. That wasn't something she liked doing in the best of times, and she typically measured or weighed all her food, closely monitoring her intake.

Driving home, I wondered if I had made the right decision. A big part of me wanted to bring Colleen home straight away and get some food into her, before she had too much time to rethink her agreement to eat. Another part of me wanted to encourage this social encounter. Hearing from concerned friends might have a greater influence on her decision-making than hearing more from me. Also, she so rarely socialized with anyone outside of the dance community, and these were kind girls who had extended themselves to her. At the same time, I knew how tenuous our agreement about the weekend was. Colleen had agreed to eat, but would she follow through? On the other hand, it was only Friday night; I still had Saturday and Sunday to get her to come around. She was not yet in physical danger. She could easily go another twelve hours without eating. Was I handling this situation in the best way possible? Would I have made a different decision with more time to think about it? I did manage to let it all go over those four miles of driving. After all, she would be back in my care in the morning.

It was a long weekend at our house. Colleen stayed in bed much of the time, which was very unusual for her. She was tired, due to eating so little, but in the past that had never stopped her from being up and dressed and in the world. She was in bed thinking. I spent a fair amount of time talking with her, and even more time giving her the space she seemed to need. I don't recall Joe talking to Colleen much that weekend; maybe he did. He often left this sort of thing to me, as these conversations had a better chance of going smoothly between us than between him and her. My background in psychotherapy most likely helped at these times.

It wasn't until late Sunday afternoon when Colleen finally came downstairs to have some toast and a glass of milk. We had been talking again, upstairs.

"Colleen, do you remember much about being in the Retreat?" I asked as she lay in bed.

"Yes, I remember all of it," she responded.

"Do you want to be back there?"

She paused.

"Maybe you do," I suggested. "Maybe it will be easier for you to get well there."

"No, I didn't like it there. I don't want to go back. I didn't like anything about it."

"What about recovering alongside Ryan? That was lucky, wasn't it? What were the chances that a boy your age would have been in that hospital with the same diagnosis as you at that time? You two became friends, helping each other to get well. You especially influenced him when you arrived and started eating. Remember? He saw your choice and decided to get off his feeding tube and eat food."

Colleen smiled. "I liked Ryan. But he won't be there now."

"No, he won't," I said.

We talked some more about her experiences at the Brattleboro Retreat, where she had been hospitalized eight years earlier. Some of her memories were good, some bad. In the end, she said, "I don't want to go back to the hospital."

"Then you need to come down to the kitchen and eat," I said. "I am going to make the call within the next hour, if you do not." I had waited long enough for her to act, and I knew she needed a firm deadline. "You miscalculated, Colleen, with this plan of yours. But even if you had been eighteen already when I realized what was happening, we would have found a way to get you the help you need. Dad and I are not going to give up on you. We are not going to watch you waste away, at any age."

Colleen chose food. She chose to eat at home. As hard as she knew it would be, she said she thought she could do it. After making sure she had eaten that first small meal, I talked with her about what was up ahead, including how I could support her. She was going to need help, to be successful. I suggested we enlist her friend Cassandra, a girl she had played the flute with since fourth grade, to see how she might feel about overseeing Colleen's lunches at school. The two ate together each day, with Colleen no longer on the bus to the dance school. Colleen, in her somewhat defeated and fragile state, said it would be easier for her if I were to ask this favor. I emailed Cassandra, who was eager to help.

I would supervise breakfast, pack a lunch for Colleen (with her input, but with my final say about how much she needed to eat), Cassandra would report to me by email later in the day that Colleen had eaten all of it, and then I would oversee dinner. It wasn't an ideal plan, with me as mother in charge, but it worked for that last month of the school year. By summer, Colleen was back on board eating her food without so much help. A disaster had been narrowly averted, but I did not imagine we were fully out of the woods. Colleen's underlying disorder of obsessive-compulsive behavior remained a big issue in her life. Her body image was a huge issue. Medications took the edge off the worst of it all but were not as effective as they often are for people with depression or anxiety. Although I knew that helping Colleen to remain healthy would be a long road ahead, I had also learned by now how to enjoy a moment of success. I learned a lot from raising Colleen, not least of which was how to live in the present and not worry about the future. I can thank her for that important life skill.

20

These Dreams of You: From the Future

February 27, 2022
Dear Colleen,

Last night you visited me from the future. Little did I know that when you left this life, you traveled fifteen years ahead. Arriving from the year 2037, in my dream, you were clearly happy and healthy, wearing the dress I made for you when you were eight, the one with a matching smaller version for your Felicity doll. That dress fit you for many years and it made sense in my dream, as odd situations sometimes do in that realm, to see you in it now. I was sitting on your bed in your former bedroom, and at first you were talking to Joe in our bedroom. I heard him asking about your life now. You told him about a movie he could watch that would give him a good idea of life in your time, but you said it may be too hard for him because the girl in the movie was a lot like you. Apparently, the protagonist was quite obsessive and compulsive. Anorexia did not come up in this dream of mine.

You came down the hall to talk with me. We sat close together, looking into each other's eyes as we spoke. Yours were so large and round, so deep blue and bright and clear. Your eyelashes were dark and long. Just like when you were young and healthy. We spoke heart to heart. I told you that of all the accomplishments of my life, raising you and Caitlin has been my best work. I told you that I have never loved more than what I have felt for you two, and I have never had more fun than I had with you two. I said that I have been blessed with a good life, a good husband, a career that I have been passionate about, but that you two have been the best of it all. I could see you take this in, and I could see that you believed me. I could see you understanding that my love for you and Caitlin has been as deep as love can be and that motherhood has defined me more than any other aspect of my life.

This visit from you was so real and so clear and so encouraging to me. I felt such a lovely connection with you. It was a gift to be able to tell you how much you have meant to me, even though I think you knew this long before you left this life. Thank you for showing up in my dream world once again, dear sweet Colleen.

21

Mass Destruction

DURING THE SUMMER OF 2008, I became quite ill with Lyme disease. My case was not detected early and, when it was finally diagnosed, I spent four days on morphine in a hospital over an hour away. I had severe roaming pain and Bell's palsy. I came home on a very expensive antibiotic administered daily through a PICC line. Joe played nurse, caregiver, and single parent. He did a great job. I continued to experience significant pain and exhaustion for a month. I alternated between sitting up for an hour and lying down for an hour. I was available to talk with my girls, but not much else. I couldn't drive at all for a couple of weeks. During the last week of my treatment, Joe and Caitlin and I spent our pre-arranged vacation week on the coast of Maine, with nursing support in the area. I was gradually feeling better and happy to spend my days in a beach chair. Colleen, at age eighteen, chose to stay home in Vermont.

Colleen was spending a lot of time with her friend Josh that summer. They had become friends during their senior year when he had started a math club at school. Josh and Colleen were both delighted to make a friend who was equally enamored with mathematics. Josh was also an athlete and would often bike the many miles from his family's home, in the next town north, to our home. He and Colleen would spend hours talking, laughing, and just hanging out. I could see that something deeper than a casual friendship was developing between them, or at least for Colleen. Initially, Josh had not yet broken up with his girlfriend, Stephanie, who was also a friend of Colleen's. Sometimes all three of them hung at our house. Ours is a small home, so I alternated between giving them the screened porch and taking it for myself.

In late August, when Joe and Cait and I returned from our week away, I immediately noticed that all photos of Colleen, including photos of her and other family members that had been placed around the house, were missing. When asked about this, she said she had them, that she had hidden them so her friends wouldn't see them.

"The ones on my dresser in my bedroom, Colleen?" I asked, with annoyance.

"Josh or Stephanie could have gone in there," she defended herself. Her voice was higher pitched than usual.

"Alright, just put them back. Today, please."

The photos did not appear. A day or two went by and I asked again. Her response was an impatient, "I'll get them!"

More days went by. Colleen wasn't home when I found myself stewing over those missing photos and decided to take matters into my own hands. I assumed the framed pictures would be simply sitting on the top of her clothes in her dresser drawers. I was close; what I found were empty frames. My stomach clenched. My muscles tightened. Fear was morphing into rage. Colleen would be home soon, and I would get to the bottom of this then. Perhaps the actual photographs were elsewhere. I tried to calm myself with the idea of this possibility.

I went about doing some household chores, but I could not easily distract myself from this development. What had she done with those photos of mine? Those were MY photographs. I had taken every one of them, and I had framed them. The ones of her in her room, photos of her as a dancer, printed to specific sizes to fit in particular frames, had been gifts from me. I hated to see them go, but they had been given and were now hers to do with what she pleased. But the photos in my bedroom? They were NOT hers to remove, hide, or worse yet, destroy! Could she have?

I managed to move on from this state of anger and angst and it was not until the next day, when Colleen was home, that I opened a photo album in the living room to see what I might find. Empty spaces, where photos of Colleen had been, was what I discovered. My heart started to pound. I pulled another album off the shelf. No photos of Colleen. None. Just glaring empty spaces where photos of her had been placed. I was astounded. I was angry. I felt assaulted. I decided I might be overreacting. The photographs could still exist, along with those missing photos from frames. I went to the kitchen to find Colleen. I stood at the end of the kitchen counter and said, "Where are the photographs, Colleen?" I was working hard to remain calm but my low, deep voice gave my emotions away.

"I'll get them, Mom!" she nearly shrieked.

"You don't have them, do you, Colleen? You don't have the photographs. You destroyed them, didn't you?" My voice was shaking now.

"Maybe."

"Oh, my god," I responded. I felt like I'd been punched in the gut. I doubled over, leaning on the countertop. I could barely breathe.

"I'm sorry, mom. I'm sorry," Colleen said. She now spoke in a voice that showed her genuine concern with my reaction. She could finally see how much her actions had hurt me. She was meek and apologetic for about a minute, maybe only a half-minute. However short the time, it was very clear that she knew she had messed up and hurt me terribly. And then, as quickly as she had apologized, she switched to defending herself. She drew herself up and said,

"I can't have people looking at photos of me when I didn't have anorexia. I can't have people looking at me when I was overweight!"

"Those were not your photographs to destroy, Colleen," I responded. I was barely able to speak. "They were mine, not yours," my voice got stronger. "The ones in your room were yours, the rest were mine. All the rest. Mine. And they can't be replaced." I had just, a few months earlier, in an effort to declutter, tossed out 20 years of photo negatives.

Colleen's quick shift to defending her behavior angered me. Upon reflection a while later, I understood that she was unable to tolerate the feeling of having hurt me so deeply. We never spoke of the photographs again. I had said what I needed to say. Further words would not bring those pictures back. I later investigated far enough to find that any photos in albums predating Colleen's first hospitalization remained untouched, with the exception of photos where she was eating something. Those were gone. My beloved photo of my girls eating ice cream on the porch in Maine, gone. And everything after age ten had been destroyed. It became impossible for me to look at those photo albums, even after her death. Having an album fall open to blank spaces, and often several blank pages in a row, broke my heart anew each time it happened, so I didn't look.

It was not until a couple of months ago, while writing these pages, that I felt brave enough to take on the project of organizing loose photos into those albums. I have received by mail, from friends going through their photos during the pandemic, some of the pictures of my girls that I had sent out. I often gave duplicate prints to friends and family, back in the days of film cameras. Having some of these photos returned to me brings great joy. My friend Susan framed a photo of my girls on the beach in Maine, taken the summer Colleen was eleven. She is holding Caitlin in her arms, with Caitlin's legs tight around Colleen's waist and her arms stretched out wide. This photograph epitomizes their relationship. And then there is the one my brother-in-law gave me of Colleen and Caitlin and her three boy cousins, all spiffed up for Easter dinner and sitting on the couch in our living room. Colleen was eleven or twelve. Rowan, her youngest boy cousin, had been clowning around in such a manner that his mother, Cynthia, was on him to stop misbehaving. He may have been saying something inappropriate or doing something physical that his mother objected to. What Caitlin most remembers of the scene is that Cynthia, between moments of speaking to Rowan, was giving stern looks to the other four children, asking them to stop encouraging him with their laughter. As my camera clicked, I captured Colleen visibly trying to contain herself while on the verge of bursting into laughter. Rowan sat in the center of the lineup with his mouth shut tight, looking straight ahead as though he was trying very hard to neither move nor speak. Who knows what he had just said? Caitlin was sheepishly looking up at her sister, grinning. She was enjoying Colleen's inability to hold it together. This, despite Colleen being the one who was most likely to acquiesce to the desires of adults. This photo came back to me from Cynthia's husband, Rod, when he was going through photographs after Cynthia's death, sixteen months after Colleen's. It sits in a frame by my bed now, a wonderful reminder of how much fun Colleen could be.

22

I Can't Keep Anything Alive!

OF ALL THAT HAPPENED IN MY LIFE WITH COLLEEN, the events of summer 2009 were arguably the most challenging and most traumatic. For years afterwards, I would count how many summers had passed since that one, calmed by that growing number. It has been four years now, I would think, four years since that summer she came so close to dying, since we came so close to losing her. Life is better now. Four years is good. The events of that summer are decidedly in the past. Colleen is doing well, or at least well enough.

Colleen had not graduated with her class in the spring of 2008. She had a couple of courses yet to complete, to gain enough credits for graduation and to complete the required number of English courses. She had missed out on completing her first semester of freshman year because of her hospitalization in Wisconsin. Those in charge at the high school had been confident that she could still finish up within the usual four years, but taking full loads of coursework was challenging for this girl with OCD. English classes were particularly difficult, with their writing requirements. So she went back to the high school that fall, for that final English course and Physics—a course of great interest to her. Those two courses kept her busy enough for a few months.

In the spring semester of that extra high school year, Colleen was all done with coursework but, because she had not officially graduated, she was still eligible to take SAT exams. She decided to teach herself what would constitute Calculus II in preparation to take the AP Calculus B/C exam. She learned the material from an old textbook lent to her by a math teacher at the high school and earned the highest score possible. There had never been any question about her math ability, and pursuing this study made her happy. Through that whole year she continued to tutor math students, privately. She had been doing this work for a few years. During the summer of 2009, however, she had far less tutoring work and her own math studies were done. Colleen had not applied to colleges because of her extreme difficulties with perfectionism and writing. She was at a bit of a crossroads, needing to figure out what was next for her. She chose anorexia.

Colleen began to lose weight fast, a talent she had honed over the years. Joe and I were, of course, very alarmed. Unlike in May of 2008, Colleen was now legally an adult, and it would be much harder for us to get her admitted to a hospital if it came to that. More importantly, a hospital program was unlikely to work for her if she did not have buy-in.

It was June, and my brother was visiting from the west coast for a week, as he did annually. He picked up where he had left off the year before, poking fun at my daughters. I used to remind him that it was not 1965 and they were not me, his younger sister, but nothing I said had ever curtailed his mirthful older-brother style of tossing disrespect their way. Perhaps because he was an adult, my girls seemed to thrive on their uncle's jokes at their expense. I credit Colleen with continuing to smile at what he said about her when she was nineteen and circling the anorexia drain again, just a few short weeks before an emergency hospitalization. Jim and I had gone to visit our cousin in Maine for a weekend. When arriving back home, Colleen was noticeably thinner than before we left. It had been good for me to get away for a couple of days, but coming home was hard. I was beside myself with worry and terribly upset with her.

Turning to Jim, just moments after we had walked in the door, I said, "Does she look worse to you?"

Looking directly at her, he responded, "She looks like she could use a meal." Always with the New Jersey sarcasm, delivered out of the corner of his mouth, and always eliciting smiles from those around him, including Colleen. Even she smiled a bit, from her illogical anorexic stance. I didn't smile; I went out to the screened porch to sit in a rocking chair and cry alone in the dark.

It fell to me, day after day, to try to get her to change her mind about what she was doing. She had still not returned to psycho-therapy. Conversations about eating between her and Joe typically did not go well.

"Colleen, you do understand where this will lead, right? You understand that if you continue to eat as little as you are eating and you continue to lose weight at this rapid pace, you will die. You know that, right?" We were talking in her bedroom.

"I know. But I need to be the thinnest person alive," she replied, daily.

"But after achieving that goal, you will die. You won't be here to feel pride in your accomplishment. I will not include anorexia in your obituary. And how do you think Dad and Caitlin and I are supposed to deal with your dying?"

"I don't know." She paused. "You won't include my cause of death?"

"No, I won't." I did include anorexia in her obituary, years later. But I told her I would not, at this time, because I was trying any-thing I could think of to get her to give up this craziness.

"Does life really not matter to you, Colleen?" I asked. "You are so talented. I know you have lost much of that, in the service of OCD, but you still have your brilliance in math and your vast knowledge and love of ballet. Don't you want to live to continue those pursuits?"

"I don't know. I don't know anymore. I mean I have to be thinner than I am now. I have to be the best anorexic alive."

"Even if it kills you?"

"Maybe. I'm not sure."

This was an exhausting conversation. We engaged in some form of it for many days. Was it weeks? I did not keep a journal, but I think this went on for weeks.

I had planted a vegetable garden that spring, as I had for decades. We can't safely put our vegetable sets into the ground until late May or early June in Vermont. There was a woodchuck in the neighborhood that year. He had been tossing my garden, relentlessly. Every time I re-planted, he came in under the cover of darkness to toss it. This animal did not eat anything. He just tossed. When I was able to get out there early enough in the morning, I could salvage most of my tender plants. Typically, one or two were too wilted to save. Once, I had to go back to the garden center to repurchase all that I had planted. The woodchuck had been ignoring the Havahart trap I had set, except for the two nights when he (or another animal) tripped it and made off with the peanut butter on cracker without getting caught.

I was sitting in the garden, not purposefully, but plopped back on my butt where I had fallen from my crouching position, when Joe pulled in. Overwhelmed with a sense of powerlessness, sitting there in a drizzly rain, I said to him as he emerged from his car and looked at me quizzically, "I can't keep anything alive!"

"I can't keep anything alive!" I cried, as our daughter starved upstairs in her bedroom.

Some of what happened that summer is blurry in my memory, some of it is crystal clear, and some of it is hearsay. For instance, I clearly recall Caitlin telling me that the next time someone asked if Colleen was her sister, she would deny it. The hearsay part is what happened in town during a Friday night Gallery Walk at the start of July. Apparently, Caitlin's friend Nick asked her if that was Colleen approaching them on the street. When Caitlin responded yes, Nick asked why she looked like she was eighty years old. While Cait no longer recalls her response, she imagines that she deflected or didn't answer. She and I both remember that when she came home that evening, she said she would now be telling anyone who asked that no, that person was not her sister. As a thirteen-year-old, she was mortified that people were noticing, judging, wondering about skeletal Colleen. She didn't know how to answer, and she didn't want to know. She decided that she would be denying any relationship in the future.

Another challenge Caitlin faced that summer was in taking the bus to town with Colleen. We live in a rural setting, but the girls could walk about a mile and a half to pick up a bus. It amazes me that Colleen was still able to walk that far, but she was never short on determination. Sometimes they would arrive just behind the bus's arrival at the stop, and Caitlin would run to catch up. She then had to hold the bus, asking the bus driver to wait for her sister who could not run. Not only did Caitlin feel embarrassed by her sister's self-imposed physical limitations, but she also overheard the bus driver saying something to Colleen one day about needing to put some weight on. Colleen had been struggling mightily to pull herself up, one step at a time, onto the bus. The bus driver was right to comment. Unfortunately, a few months later, after returning home from a long hospital stay and at a healthier weight, Colleen was no longer willing to use the bus for transportation. Her stance was that she couldn't let that bus driver see that she had gained weight.

How we got to a place where Colleen was willing to meet with Nancy, I do not recall. I imagine I played on her ambivalence, in our conversations, long enough that she finally agreed to talk to someone besides me. Colleen made the appointment. I phoned Nancy, before their meeting time, to say that I would be picking Colleen up afterwards and to ask if she would stand at the top of the stairs as Colleen descended, in case I was not yet outside the office door on the second floor of the building. I was very concerned about Colleen falling on those stairs and wanted someone to be there if that were to happen. I also told Nancy that I had set up an appointment with our family physician, for directly after Colleen and Nancy met. I warned her of Colleen's appearance, and I wanted her to know that medical intervention was in the works.

Getting into my car after her psychotherapy appointment, I told Colleen we were headed to our doctor's office. She balked, but there wasn't anything she could do about my decision. We were expected there, and I was in the driver's seat. I wanted to get Colleen to the local hospital emergency department, but I thought it would be much easier to get her to walk into a doctor's office than into an ED. At the medical office, together with our physician, it was decided that I would call Joe to meet us there; we would take her to the ED together. I told Colleen that if she resisted, Joe would simply pick her up and put her into the car. We all knew how easy that would be for him to do, given her lack of physical strength.

The time the three of us spent in the ED is etched in my memory as a nightmare. As happens in most emergency departments, we were there a long time. We were eventually met by an emergency mental health worker named Adam. He had been called in to meet with Colleen, as there was just one mental health person on-call at any given time for the whole county—a fact that shocked the professionals in a city hospital where we ended up two days later. Adam was trained to assess emergency mental health situations, but he may have had no more than a B.A. degree in English. Having worked in community mental health, I knew much about our county emergency system. Adam apparently didn't know anything about anorexia. Nor did the physician on call who eventually met with Colleen.

After a long time and many conversations (Colleen and Adam, Colleen and the doctor, the three of us and Adam), Colleen was told, in our presence, that she should go home, eat more food, drink more fluids, and follow up with her therapist. Mind you, when Colleen was admitted at a hospital in Boston about thirty-six hours later, her weight was fifty-three pounds. We were told by a psychiatrist in that ED, who said he had thirty-five years of experience in psychiatry (mostly in emergency settings), that he had never seen a living person with such a low BMI. But I am getting ahead of myself.

My response to Adam, when he relayed the message from the physician about eating and drinking and seeking psychotherapy, was this:

"You better watch the obituaries, Adam. Because in a day or two you are going to see that this young woman has died. You think that if a person doesn't have a rope or a gun, they are not a danger to themselves. She is starving to death, Adam. Starving! And death by starvation is the same as death by any other method. She is a danger to herself, and you are not stepping up to hospitalize her and keep her safe. You better watch those obits, because this one will be on you!"

I was furious. I was as angry as I had ever been in my life. Writing this, now, makes me shake with anger. But, man, was I clear in my speech. I was strong and clear, and I said what needed to be said. And then we went home. I was still enraged when we arrived, around midnight. It was going to be a while before I could go to sleep. I carried on a bit longer, beside myself with rage and frustration. I had worked so hard for so long to get that girl to a hospital, to an ED from where I was sure she would be admitted to an inpatient psych unit. I even knew where I wanted her to go and was ready to advocate for that placement. But we were sent home, and now we were back where we had been for weeks. I paced and carried on a bit longer, and when I paused, Colleen said, "I liked Adam."

"Of course, you liked Adam! Adam did what you wanted. But Adam is clueless! He has no idea what he is doing! He is way in over his head. And that doctor! Christ, has no one in this county ever heard of death by starvation?! Is this rocket science?"

Eventually, we all went to bed. The next day, Colleen and I resumed negotiations.

That trip to our local ED had been on a Thursday. Colleen and I talked all day Friday. I spoke at length with a person at an eating disorders program outside of Boston. Colleen eventually talked with that same woman, asking many questions. We did this from the screened porch. Colleen was in contemplation mode. How had I finally gotten her to this place of considering residential treatment? I had told her that I was fearful that she would fall on the stairs, hit her head, suffer a brain injury, and no longer be the same smart person she had always been. She had been struggling each evening to hoist herself up the stairs to her bedroom, with her computer under one arm, pulling herself up one step at a time, with her other hand and arm on the railing. We did not help her. We were not interested in enabling her in this way. We did not want to lighten her physical discomfort or her fear. We wanted her to deal with the natural consequences of being so emaciated, but we also worried about her safety on those stairs.

I felt that I had struck gold when Colleen perked up with concern about that head injury scenario.

"You mean I could fall, live, and not be really smart anymore?" she asked. This had not occurred to her as a possibility.

"Yes, that is exactly what I am afraid of, Colleen. And I think that is the last thing you would want, to live and not have your full cognitive capacity." Colleen's intelligence was such a big part of her identity.

It was evening by now, and the way we had left things with the treatment program in Massachusetts was that all we had to do was call in the morning to say we were on our way. Colleen was still deciding.

"Honey, I strongly recommend that you let us take you in tomorrow. With your history, I can get a judge in Brattleboro to order you into a hospital program on Monday. I have been talking to a lot of people today and I now have the name of a judge who can be counted on to do this. But I have two concerns. The first is that you will not be able to choose your program. You will be sent to the Retreat again. They can make you healthy, but they do not have an eating disorders program. You need an eating disorders program if you are to succeed in the long run. My other concern, Colleen, is that you will not make it through the weekend. You are so unsteady on those stairs. You are so physically debilitated. You aren't eating anything at all. I don't know what is going to happen over the next couple of days, but I fear the worst."

I no longer recall if Colleen agreed that night or the next morning to go to Boston. I do know that on our way out of town Saturday morning we had Caitlin in the car, having arranged to meet her friend, Lena, and Lena's mother just off an exit of the interstate in Vermont. Caitlin would spend the day and night with them. Joe was driving and I was in the front passenger seat, with the girls seated in the back.

"Does it matter to you if I die?" Colleen asked Caitlin.

Caitlin began to cry. Then, Colleen began to cry because she had upset her sister. I turned to the backseat and said, "What kind of a question is that to ask your younger sister, Colleen? How can you ask her that?"

Caitlin had asked me, perhaps a week earlier, what was going to happen to Colleen. I had told her that I didn't know, but I was

THESE DREAMS OF YOU

doing everything I could to make sure she would accept help and stop starving. I had acknowledged to Caitlin that it was possible to die from anorexia and that this *could* happen to her sister. I felt I needed to be honest with her, but I had also tried to reassure her that I was working very hard for a good outcome. Caitlin had been just five years old during Colleen's first hospitalization, so she was familiar with the anorexia beast. She more clearly recalled that second hospitalization when Colleen was fourteen and she was eight. And she could tell that this time was different; it was worse. I had less control over this situation, and Caitlin sensed that difference.

When we called the treatment center outside of Boston that Saturday morning, to say we were coming, we were told that because it was not a weekday, we would need to go through the Emergency Department of a nearby hospital. The treatment center was not staffed to do an intake on a Saturday, but it had a relationship with the hospital. After the two-and-half-hour drive from Vermont, the three of us began our long wait in the ED. When Colleen was finally seen, it was decided that she was not physically well enough to go into the treatment program we had traveled to the Boston area for. She was admitted to the hospital, in a semi-intensive care unit. We spent a long time talking with professionals in the ED before she was moved upstairs. Dressed in a gown and sitting on an examination table, Colleen was asked to lie back and then sit up, which she could not do. I noticed that she had a layer of fine hair on her back, an adaptation for survival when humans are starving. Hair helps to hold in body heat. As she was sitting on that table, her blood pressure dropped dramatically, and ED staff leapt into crisis mode. Apparently, we had gotten her to this hospital in the nick of time.

Joe and I drove home in the wee hours, arriving in Vermont around four in the morning. We were both exhausted from the day, and I had needed to stay awake to help him stay awake on that endless stretch of Route 2 in Massachusetts. We split a beer and went to sleep for a couple of hours. It was Joe's birthday a day or two later, so it must have been a month or more that Colleen had been tanking at home. We were glad to have her in a safe place, but we knew, from having her in hospitals in the past, that we all had a long road ahead of us.

23

Boston

COLLEEN SPENT SIX DAYS at Mount Auburn Hospital, with a person sitting in her room around the clock. I visited her there, a few days in. She was not just emaciated but very weak. I found it heartbreaking to see not just how physically frail she had become but also how defeated she seemed to feel. She was fearful of walking to the bathroom on her own. And her spirit was weak; she presented as a meek and terrified person with severe illness. She was a mere shell of the daughter I knew. I met with a social worker, who felt that Colleen's fear of walking was based on her emotional reaction to being in the hospital, rather than physical limitation. Although I had never seen anything like this in my daughter before, I understood the phenomenon. It was all incredibly hard for me to witness. I felt so sad, more so for her than for myself. I wept quietly by her bedside as she slept.

A few days after my visit, when it was decided that she was physically well enough to be moved to the psychiatric unit at Tufts Medical Center, she was discharged from Mount Auburn but not immediately transported. In fact, she sat for hours in her room with no medical attention. When my close friend, Sarah, having heard from me that Colleen would be on the move that day, telephoned her to ask how she was feeling about the move, Colleen wasn't making a lot of sense. Sarah alerted me and I called Colleen, who reported sitting on her bed, dressed and ready to go, for what had felt like a long time already. She was able to communicate with me, but she sounded quite confused. I don't recall how long it took for me to reach someone at the hospital who would take charge and get to the bottom of what was going on. As it turned out, Colleen's electrolytes were way out of balance, but no one knew this because she had been disconnected from all monitors. Colleen's care had slipped through the cracks of a busy hospital unit after her official discharge, despite an ambulance not arriving to transport until hours later. From my home in Vermont, I spent those hours on the phone, which was all I could do. That evening, around 9:00, I received a call from the doctor who had managed to get the situation resolved. He was calling from his home to reassure me that Colleen had been moved successfully. I thanked him profusely.

It was about three in the morning when my phone rang again. I took the call downstairs so as not to wake Joe. We had both been lacking adequate sleep for far too many nights. It was Colleen on the telephone. She told me she was lying on top of a bed, fully dressed, and she didn't know what was going on. I asked some questions: Was there anyone around at all? A roommate? Hospital staff? Did she know where she was? Did she know how she got there? She couldn't answer anything definitively. I told her I would get help.

I called the main line at Tufts Medical Center and was put through to the psychiatric unit. I got someone to go in and check on her, and I received a call back shortly afterwards. I was told, when I first got through, that Colleen hadn't responded to questions upon arrival. She had said nothing at all and had been assessed as noncompliant. I explained what had happened that day, that she had gone for hours without medical attention and had been suffering confusion before she had even left Mount Auburn

Hospital. I was incredulous that I needed to intervene in this way. What goes on for people who have no advocate? What happens to patients who have no one to call at three in the morning?

Colleen was moved to a medical floor at Tufts, as she was clearly not ready to be without that level of care. She spent three days on that floor, where her medical situation could be closely watched. In addition to her electrolytes being out of balance, she was experiencing refeeding syndrome. Her symptoms of refeeding included confusion, weakness, fatigue, and edema. This last symptom was extremely challenging for Colleen, emotionally; puffy ankles do not sit well with people with anorexia nervosa. Her symptoms could have been worse, though, something I realize now as I look up this syndrome on the internet. It was probably better that I knew less back then.

Colleen would later tell me, when I visited her on the psych unit, that when she was in the ambulance, traveling from Mount Auburn to Tufts, she wanted to ask questions, she wanted to talk, but she couldn't seem to form the words to speak. She said that she felt so unwell both physically and mentally, so not herself, so out of control, that she thought she was going to die "in this ambulance, somewhere in Boston, with my parents in Vermont." I was severely struck by her level of aloneness when she told me this, and I felt humbled to learn that we mattered that much to her, that when she thought she was on her way out of this life, she was concerned about Joe and me not being there. This may sound like a typical concern for a young person, but remember, this girl had been at odds with us about her right to do what she chose with her body and her life, for many years. That summer we had experienced the worst of her shutting out our help, our concern, our desire to keep her alive. For her to report what she had experienced in that ambulance was monumental in moving me towards even deeper compassion for this daughter I loved so fiercely and had been trying so hard to protect for so long.

About every five days, throughout her two months in Boston, I drove three hours from our home to Tufts, visited Colleen for a few hours, and drove back home. On one of these visits, perhaps a week or two into her stay, I arrived at the hospital for a planned meeting. I was escorted to a conference room where members of Colleen's treatment team filed in, one at a time. Colleen arrived as well. All were cordial, if not welcoming, towards me. Dr. Hsu, the psychiatrist who headed the unit, was not yet present. We waited briefly and then someone else on the team began the meeting, informally.

The purpose of the meeting was to update me on the progress of Colleen's treatment and for team members to ask me a few questions. All seemed curious to hear from me about Colleen's history, despite all they knew from talking with her. I talked a bit about the onset of her anorexia, her earlier hospitalizations, and her outpatient treatment. With Colleen's approval, I passed around a photo of her at a healthy weight. She was a beautiful girl, and the staff was surprised to see what she would look like at a normal weight. Then their questions began. Their queries seemed reasonable and gently posed at first, and then someone asked me if I had told Colleen, when she was nine, that it was always a thin girl who got to dance the part of Clara in *The Nutcracker* in our town. I was caught up short by this question. I slowly responded that I didn't know, that I didn't recall saying that, that I *may* have said such a thing, but I didn't in that moment have a memory of a conversation like that.

All eyes were on me, as I spoke, and I realized I was being interrogated about my role in Colleen's mental illness. Despite this not being my first experience with the mother-blaming that often occurs when a girl has anorexia, I was incredulous. And then I was angry. As I opened my mouth to say something like, "You don't actually think that my mothering is at the root of

Colleen's obsessive-compulsive symptoms or her anorexia?" the doctor entered the room, and all eyes shifted to him. The body language in the room instantly changed. Those who had been leaning forward in interrogation mode with me sat back. No one spoke as he sat and addressed me.

"We haven't seen much of you around here," commented Dr. Hsu.

"That's because I live in Vermont and I have another, younger child," I replied. I was feeling ready for him, perhaps primed by what had occurred just before he had walked in. I was astounded by the shift in the energy in the room and annoyed that I did not get a chance to question the motive behind what I had been asked before he arrived. *They may be afraid of Dr. Hsu,* I thought, *but I am not.* I managed to remain cordial, if not polite, as a rottweiler pulled at its chain inside of me. I saw the way in which those who seemed confident and outspoken moments earlier now deferred to the psychiatrist. I was observing a hierarchy that had annoyed me in the past, one that is common in a psychiatric setting, but had never made me this mad. Still, I silenced Rottweiler Ann and listened to what the doctor said about Colleen's progress in treatment.

I did, during that meeting and otherwise, feel that Colleen was in good hands at Tufts. Dr. Hsu was a firm believer in treating severe eating disorders in a unit with patients with other psychological challenges. He felt that an eating disorders program was a great place for patients to collude with others in cheating their way out of compliance. I could see his point, especially having spoken to a local parent of a girl who had spent some time in the program we had initially traveled to Boston for. That conversation happened after we had gotten Colleen into Mount Auburn Hospital and were still exploring her placement for eating disorder treatment. As it turned out, the psych unit at Tufts was a good place for Colleen to get well, as she followed the rules and gained weight there. She made a friend, another nineteen-year-old, who was in the hospital with a different presenting problem. This girl was more likely after a safe place to sleep, to avoid homeless shelters, than truly in need of psychiatric care. Bethany had some fun ideas for craft projects, such as decorating everyone's door, and that friendship enriched Colleen's time on that unit. While Bethany wasn't there nearly for as long as Colleen was, they formed a bond and remained friends afterwards; Colleen later visited her for a weekend in Boston. Today Bethany is thriving.

Colleen's weight was so low when she was first admitted to the hospital that it took two months to bring it up to a place where it would be safe to discharge her, despite not yet being at the weight goal that had been set up. From her discharge plan:

. . . *Since admission she has been gaining weight slowly and has been 100% compliant with her treatment plan and diet . . . Her calories were continually increased to continue her weight gain and they are currently at 3400 per day. Her goal weight is 92 lbs. where she has agreed to stay forever. Patient's insurance will run out on 9/16. Although staff has stated her OCD symptoms appear better, patient states that she does not believe her OCD is better, but that she is better at hiding it. She feels conflicted because she will follow her plan to stay at 92 lbs., but she still desires to be anorexic, and this conflict will cause her to be unhappy. She is currently at 83.7 lbs. on 9/16.*

Colleen came home underweight. I had fought hard to get added time from our medical insurance company, so Colleen had been at Tufts weeks longer than insurance initially allowed. In the end, they set a limit that didn't seem realistic to me. The chances of Colleen's success out of hospital were questionable. To have to eat as many calories as needed, without the strict rules and support of a hospital setting, was a stretch for anyone recovering from anorexia. At the same time, I was happy to have her come home. The academic year had begun, and I was back to teaching full time at the undergraduate college where I worked. In her first week or so at home, I was able to arrange my schedule to be home at lunchtime, or Colleen would go to work with me. She needed someone to oversee her eating. Before Colleen had left the hospital, Nancy had found a group after care program for Colleen to attend. As soon as a space was open there, I began taking Colleen to it and picking her up, daily. This meant an extra hour or so of driving for me each day, but the program seemed like a good idea. She soon found someone to ride along with, from our town, which lightened my load. A former student of mine, one of my best from the years I trained graduate level mental health counselors, ran the program. Therese is a smart and talented psychotherapist, so I knew Colleen was in good hands. Participants had a wide range of diagnoses, and at first it seemed like a good fit for Colleen. She attended for a couple of weeks before giving it up. She decided it wasn't helpful enough to continue; unfortunately, this left her at home alone for a good part of every weekday.

Colleen struggled, mightily, with her ambivalence about gaining weight that fall. She tried hard to keep busy, to keep from thinking about how much to eat. She sometimes helped me with tasks around the house, something she hadn't done much of in the past. I generally begin to decorate the house for Christmas over the weekend following Thanksgiving, and Colleen asked if she could help that year. We set up our miniature winter village together, which I think about every year now as I set it up alone again. I enjoyed her company in that task and was aware how hard it was for her to have free time. I was glad to help her fill some of that time, so she wouldn't use it perseverating about her eating and her weight. She was trying hard to do what was asked of her, regarding her diet, despite not fully buying in.

Then, with her weight up around eighty-eight pounds—yes, she had successfully gained weight at home—she menstruated. Underweight women do not menstruate, and it had been months since Colleen had done so. This was a sign that she was returning to a healthy weight. She at once started restricting her diet again. Colleen did not talk about this. I simply saw it. She bled on a sheet and tossed it away in a garbage can in the basement, not wanting me to know about it. She scaled back on her calories. Colleen was meeting with Nancy, weekly, and she was back to tutoring. She was visiting my mother in a nursing home in town a few times a week. She was continuing to stay as busy as she could, but that goal of weighing 92 pounds was just too unpalatable for her. The closer she got to it, the more she bargained, redoing the math according to information she found online about body mass index, calculating that she (with her slight build and standing only four feet ten inches tall) should not have to weigh that much. Colleen had stunted her growth in her early adolescence, by con-tinually holding her weight back until just before the date of a new weight goal. Now she was struggling to come to terms with weighing what professionals said she must, at her short height, as an adult. This struggle would continue to plague her for a long while, until her mid-twenties when she would completely give up on making any effort to comply with healthy weight expectations.

24

Gloria

MY MOTHER, GLORIA, and Colleen had a close relationship for most of Colleen's life, with my mother passing away just two years before Colleen did. Colleen visited Gloria in the nursing home when she was nineteen not just to keep busy, but because she genuinely cared for her grandmother.

Colleen was sixteen months old when my mother, still living in New Jersey that September, entered a deep depression and attempted suicide. I received a phone call about this incident from a hospital and wondered how I had missed this depression of hers when I had seen her for an afternoon a few weeks earlier. This was not Gloria's first major depression and suicide attempt, but this time managing the fallout from it was on my shoulders alone. My parents had been divorced for many years and my brother lived on the west coast.

Gloria's situation was a lot for me to manage from Vermont, with two half time jobs and a toddler at home. After the suicide attempt, she was no longer welcome in her previous living situation in another woman's home, and she needed a plan. I traveled to New Jersey for a few days, with Colleen in tow, to visit my mother and begin to figure out next steps. Later, back in Vermont, I spent many hours on the phone with psychiatrists and New

Jersey officials who wanted me to take her into my home. This I was not willing to do. I asserted that my mother would ruin my marriage, not to mention that my family of three was living in a small four room apartment at the time. I felt willing to do all I could to find a good living situation for Gloria, short of housing her myself. I felt badly, for her, that this was my stance, but I did not succumb to feeling any guilt over it.

So Gloria stayed put in a state facility until I could manage to find her a place to live. She had been wanting to move to Vermont to be closer to my family, so I focused my energies locally. By November I managed to secure a place for her in a small town about a half hour from us. My brother, Jim, flew east from Seattle for Thanksgiving and helped me move her from New Jersey to a newly opened community housing situation for people in transition in Vermont. Gloria seemed pleased enough with this arrangement, and I felt a tremendous sense of relief after getting her moved in. She seemed to be on the mend, with this move closer to us. She lived there for a year and a half before moving into a subsidized apartment of her own in that same town. That later move to her own apartment brought her great joy. Gloria went on to become active in her community and did well for many years. I think that the years she spent living alone in that apartment, retired from paid work, with my family in her life and involvement in her community, may have been the happiest years of her long life. Becoming close to her granddaughter, Colleen, was no small part of this.

Gloria had been a good mother to me when I was growing up. She had not managed to keep me safe from a sometimes-violent father, but she did love me and take care of me and my brother in many other ways. I don't think I could have been such a good parent to my own children if I had not been well-parented myself, even if only by one of the two adults in the family. While there were some big problems in my family, and both of my parents were limited in some significant ways, I felt mostly well-cared for by my mother. I recall doing a fun art project with my brother and her, one Christmas season. I recall having a good time shopping for clothes with her. And she smiled at us. Later, during our adolescent years, my brother and I came to see her as the judgmental person she often was, but when we were young she was a mother who smiled at us often enough that we felt loved.

When I was in college, Gloria shifted to being someone I needed to support emotionally. Her first suicide attempt occurred my junior year when I was away at school, something I would learn about a few weeks later when home for Thanksgiving. Gloria would tell me the story herself, and I would feel deep sadness that she had felt so desperate.

Jim and I, at the end of that summer, helped her move out from living with our father, who had been physically abusive towards all of us on and off over the years. The way that decision went down is not a happy memory. In August, a couple of weeks before I was to return to school, there was a scene that took place in our kitchen that became etched in the memories of Gloria, Jim, and me. My father, Austin, became very upset with my mother about something. No one remembers those particulars. He was known for his bad temper and, although he did not always resort to violence, he often did. On that day he was yelling and threatening my mother in a scary way, clearly revving up towards physical abuse (something all three of us were hypervigilant about recognizing) when my brother stepped in. I was twenty years old, and Jim was twenty-two. He no longer lived at home, but he was present that day. He stood up to our father, telling Austin he would have to go through him first, that he was not going to allow him to hurt our mother anymore.

This was a monumental shift in the power dynamic in our

household. The three of us had been cowering and hiding from Austin's temper for as long as we had been a family. Jim later reported to me how terrified he had felt; he had had no way of knowing if Austin would reach for a drawer and pull out a knife. Instead, Austin seemed shocked by my brother's behavior and backed down.

On the day I was to return to college, in early September, Austin went with me on the two-hour trip. I did the driving on the way out, as he would be driving his car back home alone that same afternoon, after helping me to unload my belongings. The plan was for Jim to help Gloria move in with some friends, her location unknown to Austin, until an apartment she had procured would become available. Jim and I had helped her with all these arrangements. I drove too fast, in my angst, and got a speeding ticket. I recall trying to hurry my father along, to return home to New Jersey, after we had unpacked the car. He wanted to take a nap in my dorm room. The whole situation was terribly anxiety-provoking for me. To know that my mother was fleeing, to know that I was essentially keeping my father occupied so that could happen, to know that I was an accomplice in changing his life so dramatically—it was a lot. Because my brother was helping my mother move to a friend's home, she wasn't packing much, just her clothing. I knew that task would be easily accomplished in the five hours it took my father to travel with me to my college and back home again. I wanted him gone so I could be done with my part in all of this.

I had told my mother, in August, that she may as well move because I could not return to that home where my father lived. His behavior that summer had been the last straw for me; I was old enough to be no longer willing to go along with the status quo, and I wanted my mother out of harm's way as well. My brother agreed that she had to get out, that we didn't want to leave her there in this volatile and sometimes violent relationship. I am certain that Gloria never would have made this move without our support.

Gloria went back to Austin a couple of months later, for financial reasons, just as her apartment finally became available. She had not been given the additional hours promised to her at her workplace. Gloria worked part time as a clerk in a department store, with wages not suited to independent living. So, in the end, she went back to him. Austin and Gloria phoned me, at my dormitory on a Sunday evening, to tell me they had reconciled. My father did most of the talking, all upbeat that they were back together and that I was not to worry about anything. I was incredulous. I knew that I did not know the full story, I wanted to talk to just my mother, and I felt not just disappointed but angry. I had a single dorm room that year and I hung out for hours listening to music. My friend Beth joined me and listened to me trying to make sense of it all.

Gloria attempted suicide the next day. She spent a week in a hospital. She did not tell me about this until I was home for Thanksgiving, a month or so later. Gloria asked me then if I would spend the following summer at home. A summer under the same roof with my father was the last thing I wanted, but I did it for her. She needed me, and I stepped up.

Gloria loved children, and once she was settled in Vermont, in 1991, she delighted in her granddaughter. She had visited every few months since Colleen had been born, despite the drive, so they knew each other by the time she made her permanent move to Vermont. They went on to become close friends. One late August afternoon, I left my daughter in my mother's care to see as couple of clients at my office. When I arrived home, she told me that she had managed to get our so-called sliding door to move along its tracks, something she had typically not been very successful with. (This wooden door needed to be lifted slightly and carefully eased along. It was old and in need of a new track.) As Gloria had opened the door, two-year-old Colleen had said, "Gamma [Colleen did not pronounce r's], you can do that now because you just had a birthday." My mother was as tickled by the things that came out of Colleen's mouth as Joe and I were.

Colleen was four years old when I was at a dental appointment and she was in the waiting room with my mother. She had been quietly playing with some toys for nearly an hour when the receptionist said to Gloria, "She's very good." Colleen looked up from her play and offered, "I have my moments!" Perhaps her comment was more an example of self-knowledge, but both my mother and the receptionist found it amusing, and I tended to think, when it was told to me, that Colleen had meant to amuse. My mother found it delightful to spend time with this girl. Who wouldn't have?

Gloria joined forces with my mother-in-law to take care of both Colleen and her cousin Oakley, two days a week, when the children were toddlers and my sister-in-law and I were both at work. Cynthia somehow managed to coordinate her work schedule with mine that year to make this happen. The cousins got to spend time together and benefit from the loving attention of two grandmothers.

When Colleen was a bit older, she occasionally spent overnights at Gloria's apartment so Joe and I could enjoy some time together without our child. Our wedding anniversary is on New Year's Eve, and when Caitlin was just one year old and Colleen was six, she gladly went off to Gloria's for the night, leaving Joe and Caitlin and me to spend a quiet evening at home. It was delightful to enjoy time in each other's company, with just one non-verbal baby. We had an adult meal that I cooked, with Caitlin joining us at the table in her high-chair, and we danced in the living room, taking turns holding our laughing baby. Six-year-old Colleen was clever and funny, but she never stopped talking. Thanks to my mother's positive relationship with Colleen, everyone got to spend a fun evening, with Joe and me getting a break from the usual center of attention in our family.

Gloria and Colleen remained close throughout Colleen's childhood, until my mother became critical of everyone around her, a symptom of periodic depression throughout her life. Her relationship with Colleen began to erode as she criticized Colleen's hair, clothing, the way she spoke to her sister, almost everything about her. None of us were immune to her criticisms one August evening when we celebrated Gloria's birthday with gladiolas from my garden (grown for her each year, as her mother had always presented them at her birthday celebration when she was young), homemade blueberry pie (her favorite August dessert), cards and gifts. It was during this dinner at our home when I realized I needed to get her some help. Rather than appreciating the efforts that had been made to celebrate her birthday, she criticized each of us in turn. Finding help for Gloria was easier than in the past when we had lived in different states. This time, when she was eighty years old, I was there to witness her depression and get her in to see a psychiatrist before she circled the drain. Managing Gloria's depression at that time was challenging for me, in that Colleen was thirteen that summer, three years into her life as a girl with OCD and anorexia and struggling with escalating obsessive-compulsive symptoms. But, at least, my mother lived locally, and I could see what was happening with her before she tanked into suicidal behavior.

Gloria's physical health soon took a turn for the worse as well. She had suffered numerous small strokes in her seventies, which left her with poor balance. A year or so after Gloria had fallen into depression and Colleen was in the hospital in Wisconsin, Gloria took a physical fall in her apartment. Her depression was well-managed with medication at this point, but she was beginning to fail physically. After a stint in the local hospital, she spent some time in a rehabilitation facility about a half hour north of us. On an early December day when nine-year-old Caitlin was home with a stomach bug, I needed to go see my mother, and I had a phone call scheduled with hospital staff in Wisconsin. I left Caitlin alone in our rural home (something we had not done before), with lots of reassurance and my cell phone number, took the Wisconsin hospital call on the road to the rehab hospital, lost that call as I traveled north in a valley with poor cell reception, visited my mother and spoke with her rehab staff, and then headed south. As I entered Brattleboro, my phone rang. It was Caitlin, in tears, because she had called me multiple times but her calls hadn't gone through. I felt terrible about this. I told her I was parking the car to make a quick stop in the library for some books for her and I would be home very soon. I was feeling pulled in so many directions. Everyone seemed to need me at once, and I felt exhausted by it all. Although I wasn't always able to keep all plates spinning in the air, I did manage to keep them from breaking. I told myself this was something.

Gloria would go on to experience multiple falls, always resulting in phone calls from hospital staff to me during the night. She sometimes spent time in rehab centers after hospital stays. She was in a large hospital, over an hour away, for a couple of weeks after one fall that involved a brain bleed. With my only sibling living on the west coast, managing her health crises fell to me. It was after that fall, and another less serious one that soon followed and landed her in the hospital again, that I managed to finally talk her into moving to an assisted care facility in the town I live in. She was reluctant to give up her apartment and her independence but, from a hospital bed, she ultimately agreed that it was time. She spent some time in a nursing home while I searched for an assisted living placement for her.

I went to great lengths to carefully pack Gloria's things and set them all up in her new room, as close to the way it was before the move as I could manage. I took note of where she had placed things on her dresser, for instance. My mother had never been diagnosed with OCD, but it had been clear to me for some time that this disorder of Colleen's had its genetic roots in my side of the family. The day after my mother moved, she called to tell me to get her apartment back. She hated the food (a common enough complaint for elders moving into care facilities), and things were not in the right place on her dresser. Gloria had never handled change well, and she had always been the first to admit this, but this was worse than previous displays of inflexibility. I tried to remain patient (not easy, after all I had done to move her things for her and with most of her apartment still left for me to contend with), but I firmly told her that what was done was done, and she was going to have to adjust. She was furious with me for many days. This is a common enough story, but it was especially exhausting for me given all else I was also dealing with in parenting a fifteen-year-old with mental illness.

Gloria would spend over ten years in residential facilities, five and a half years in that assisted living home, and another five in a local nursing home. I visited at least weekly (daily for several weeks when she first moved to the nursing home), and Colleen went through a period of visiting her grandmother in the nursing home a few days a week. Colleen was nineteen and not long out of that lengthy hospital stay in Boston when she took a job teaching pre-calculus to her friend Sophia at the high school. After tutoring Sophia, she would walk over to the nursing home to see Gloria. Colleen was happy to have something more to do with her time, before taking the bus home. She was struggling in a big way with the urge to lose weight again, so keeping busy was very helpful to her. Tutoring and visiting her grandmother provided extensive time in her day when she could not perseverate about her weight or her eating. Gloria was delighted to have these visits from her beloved granddaughter. Their relationship had returned to a loving one after my mother's depression had been treated successfully with medication, years earlier.

As Gloria aged into her nineties and moved into the dementia program, it seemed that she had trouble telling the difference between my daughters. During my mother's last years, Caitlin occasionally visited with me, and it was our impression that Gloria experienced the granddaughter who accompanied me as an amalgam of the two. All that mattered to me was the huge smile on my mother's face when a granddaughter came to see her. In Colleen's later years she didn't visit anymore, which I felt was just as well given how emaciated she had become. Gloria had no idea how badly Colleen was doing as she approached her own death two years before Colleen died. I was glad that Gloria went first, as I couldn't imagine telling my mother that Colleen had passed away.

25

Hopes and Dreams

COLLEEN KEPT HER MATH TUTORING PRACTICE throughout the winter and spring that followed her hospital stay in Boson. She also did the books for a local business. We talked about the possibility of her taking some courses at a community college just south of us in Massachusetts. After a few weeks of on-again off-again discussion, she told me she couldn't do it, she could not go to college. She was standing at the end of the dining room table, at her computer, where she spent almost all her time when at home. She told me that the demands of college classes would be too much for her. Her perfectionism would get in her way, as it had in high school. I was not surprised, but I was disappointed. As she spoke, I knew she was right. But while I honored her self-knowledge and respected her choices about what she knew she could or could not take on, I was always sad to see another one of her dreams evaporate. She had lost so much already, and now she was letting go of a dream I had gingerly held onto, that she would be able to pursue a career in math through higher education. She had wanted that, which had motivated her to take that second level AP calculus exam less than a year earlier. But there it went, the hope of going to college gone, like so many other dreams of hers. This moment was hard for me. I did, however, feel some relief that this decision would spare us the many challenges that having her in school again would have inevitably brought. The question in my mind was what she would end up being able to do for work, with just a high school diploma.

That summer, Colleen got lucky. She was offered a job at Omega Optical, a local company manufacturing optical filters. An employee at Omega knew of Colleen's strong analytical skills because she had tutored his daughter when they were in high school. When she started at Omega she worked as a spectroscopist, but she soon moved into working in research and data analysis. Colleen was considered a strong asset to the research and development team, and I hoped she would stay with this company for many years. I knew people who had worked there for a long time, so this seemed very possible to me. She was also not the only quirky person on staff. It seemed like a good fit for her. Joe and I were delighted, as was she.

Colleen was twenty years old when she took that job, but it would be another three years before she moved to her own apartment in town. She made the decision to move because she was tired of being under my watchful eye around her eating and weight. Shortly before she announced her move to an apartment above the food co-op in Brattleboro, I met her in the kitchen early one morning to comment on the smell of her breath, that ketosis smell again. The skirt I had made not long before was falling off her hips and I had a feeling she was once again burning muscle, not fat.

"You are losing too much weight, Colleen. I can smell it."

"Leave me alone. This is my own business, not yours," she answered with annoyance.

This was what spurred her decision to move, but we were all happy with it. Joe and I both felt it was time Colleen move out to her own place, for her development as an adult and to allow Caitlin her senior year at home without her sister as the central focus in the family. While she was managing to stay out of hospitals, Colleen still had anorexia and severe OCD. Life with her was never smooth and easy. For Caitlin, this meant that when she came home in the evening after a long day at school and then dance classes, she had to contend with a curious and persistent sister. Colleen would stand in the doorway to Caitlin's room, asking endless questions about what had gone on at the dance school that day. Caitlin would try to be patient, but she had homework to do, and Colleen's questions were relentless. She never seemed satisfied with the amount of information she gleaned from Caitlin, always asking for more.

For our part, Joe and I looked forward to freedom from Colleen's constant presence in our dining room. When not at work, Colleen stood at the end of the dining room table on her laptop computer. She always wore black, nothing but black; apparently the color black can make a person look thinner. Thin, thinner, thinnest was what she was all about. Colleen inserted herself into most conversations that happened in the house, often sharing her rigid perspectives on whatever anyone was talking about. Caitlin would enjoy a more relaxed senior year of high school with her sister on the other side of town, Joe and I would come home to a more relaxed atmosphere at the end of each workday, and I could stop in to see Colleen often enough to know if she was in real trouble with weight loss.

Colleen had developed a close relationship with a male co-worker, during those years she worked at Omega. Chris helped her move her things from our home to her apartment. She wanted little help from us. I did help her find a couple pieces of furniture at a resale shop in town; Chris also helped her make a few purchases. I loved that she had this relationship with him. It was clear to me, from the way she talked about Chris, that she was smitten, and they spent a lot of time together outside of work. Colleen spoke of Chris, but she did not allow us to meet him. For a long time, years, what I made of this was that she had talked of us as though we did not understand her, and she had conveyed to him that we had repeatedly tried to block her from taking charge of her own life. She needed to portray us as the bad guys, and she couldn't risk his making a different decision about us. I don't know for sure when their relationship began, perhaps in 2012, but I did not meet him until 2016. Once, during those years, when she and Chris attended a dance performance in Brattleboro that Carrie and I also attended, Colleen insisted ahead of time that I promise not to approach them. She had a very strong need to keep us apart. Colleen and Chris sat in the front row of the large theater, with Carrie and I sitting about halfway back. During intermission, Carrie approached them to talk with Colleen, and I stood where I could at least get a glimpse of Chris. He was clean cut with a very pleasant face, as far as I could see. As tiresome as it was to me that Carrie was allowed to meet Chris while I was not, I did not find this to be out of character for Colleen. She had a significant need to control situations and people in her life, particularly me. I was glad that Colleen had found a good person to be in a relationship with, but I also would have loved to have met him.

Colleen lived in her apartment in town for about a year and half, before giving it up to move in with Chris. While she lived in her apartment, I visited her on Saturday mornings and cleaned her place for her while she talked to me about her life. I cleaned because she did not. She wanted a clean apartment, but the tasks of cleaning were beyond her, due to her perfectionism. She was no longer taking medications, some of which had taken the edge off her obsessive-compulsive symptoms, but none of which had cured her problems and all of which came with undesired side effects. For one thing, some medications (for instance, the atypical antipsychotics) made her sleepy. She wasn't as mentally sharp on them, and this was hard for her to abide. I didn't mind cleaning for her; there wasn't much to it, and it gave me something to do while she talked obsessively. From Colleen's apartment, I would drive a few blocks up the road to visit my mother in the nursing home where she was living. I called it the Canal Street Run.

In the spring of 2014, after four years on the job and less than one year in her apartment, Colleen was let go at Omega. She didn't tell me this right away, not for a few weeks, but when she did, I could hear over the telephone that she was weepy. A new couple of CEOs had been hired the previous fall, and one of them did not like her. He had taken her more challenging work away, leaving her with mundane tasks. Colleen did not do well with mundane tasks. Her obsessive-compulsive symptoms did not get in her way when she had challenging work, but when given tedious tasks to do, she fumbled. She recognized that she was slow in getting her work in, and she knew it was due to her OCD, but she was unable to change that. She was also very unhappy with the level of work she was tasked with. Eventually, she was fired. She told me it was clear that the CEO had set her up to fail because he didn't want her around. He hadn't liked her personality. It all seemed terribly unfair, to her and to me. Despite knowing that things like this often happen in workplaces, I was very disappointed for her that she had lost this job.

When Colleen told me this, it had been weeks since she had lost her job, and she had not yet applied for unemployment. I got involved helping her to do that. I also helped her with applying for work elsewhere. I drove her to another manufacturing company in town so she could hand them a cover letter and resume. The receptionist asked her to fill out an application on the spot. Colleen asked if she could take it with her and mail it in, and the receptionist said no. Colleen told her she would come in again when she had more time. Back in the car, she told me she could never fill out an application in the waiting room. They would see how long it took her, and secondly, she was certain she wouldn't be able to accomplish the task under the pressure of doing it there.

I began to feel hopeless about Colleen's work situation. She had been having a terrible time filling out her work search reports for the employment office each week; Joe had been helping her with that, and it had not been going well. I had spent countless hours working on her cover letter with her, for that one job application. Chris had taken on helping her with her resume. Each piece took hours and hours, despite all the help. We all talked with her about where else she might apply, including a company about thirty miles north. Transportation would be challenging, but there could be other employees to travel with. She never got as far as applying there. The debacle in the reception area at GS Precision had hindered her confidence that she could work. What had happened in the last months at Omega weighed on her as well. With just a high school diploma, she would start at the bottom at a new job, with some simple tasks, before being given a chance to move up. She would not do well with simple tasks.

I was on the phone with Colleen, one day while I was at work, fielding concerns about that cover letter that we had already spent hours on.

"I have to go, Colleen."

"Wait, we're not done," she responded.

"I have an appointment now, Colleen. I told you when we got on the phone twenty minutes ago that I had a 12:30 appointment. I need to get off the phone now."

"But when can we talk again? When can we finish this conversation?" She sounded a bit frantic now.

"I think we have covered what we need to cover here, Colleen. We have gone over all of it several times. I am busy, honey. I can't obsess with you about this letter. It's done. It's good. It's ready to go."

I did not have an appointment. I had plenty of work to do, but I did not have a 12:30 appointment. I had begun making up appointments at the start of our phone calls, to set time limits. Her obsessive-compulsive symptoms were driving me crazy. They were driving Joe crazy. I could only begin to imagine what it must feel like to be her. I repeatedly reminded myself of that, whenever I was at my wit's end.

I had been hired to teach a three-week course in the Netherlands that June, so I was able to escape all this stressful support of Colleen for a while. I regretted leaving Joe alone to help her with her on-going plight with the unemployment forms, and I loved getting away. A break from Colleen was hard to come by, and I was ready for one. I told Joe that if my mother died, he was to put her on ice. I would return when I was due back in three weeks, in time for Caitlin's high school graduation.

At the end of that calendar year, with Colleen's unemployment benefits having run out, she let her apartment go and moved in with Chris at his home in New Hampshire. This made sense financially, with her out of an income, and it meant he could do much less driving for them to spend time together. When she had moved to her apartment in Brattleboro, I had held hopes that Caitlin would go in to visit, watch dance movies with Colleen, even spend a night now and then, as Colleen had purchased a couch that pulled out to a bed. But none of that ever happened. Colleen never unpacked her books to place on the bookcase she bought, because that task was beyond her. She would have had to decide how to arrange them. She left almost all her belongings in boxes. She never put her clothes in the drawers of the beautiful chest she bought upon moving in. These sorts of mundane tasks were all beyond what she could manage, with her level of perfectionism. In her mind, there was one right way to do anything, and short of knowing exactly what that was, she did nothing at all.

As her mother, it was my job to hold hope for Colleen. I came to this easily, being an optimistic person by nature. When she was hospitalized at the age of ten, a co-worker told me about the daughter of a friend who had struggled with anorexia at almost as young an age. When I asked how that now twenty-year-old was doing and the answer was that she had been in and out of hospitals throughout her adolescence and was still not doing well, I was sure that would not happen to Colleen. I had held great hopes that she would be successful in overcoming her mental illness.

As Colleen was growing up and showing so much promise intellectually, I was certain she would go to college.

When Colleen needed more time at the in-patient psych unit at Tufts and our insurance company granted it with the stipulation that they would not pay for another psychiatric hospitalization for her over the years she remained on our policy, I was not concerned. In my mind, this was it; this was the last time she would go low enough with her weight to need to be in a hospital.

When she was hired at Omega Optical, I assumed she had found a job she would keep for many years.

When it was clear to me that Colleen would not become a mother, not with such severe body image issues and an inability to maintain a weight high enough to menstruate, I was sure she would be a loving aunt to Caitlin's future child or children.

When Colleen moved in with Chris and their relationship seemed solid, I hoped this would be something she could count on for a long time.

I held hopes for Colleen, every step of the way, despite so many of her and my dreams falling away, until it became clear to me that she would die young.

26

Pivot

Two and a half years before Colleen died, I stopped trying to save her. Colleen didn't want to be saved. She had lived with anorexia for fourteen years at that time. I had spent all those years supporting her in her recovery. She sometimes accepted help, and she sometimes fought it. She had always been ambivalent, at best, about recovering.

My transition to respecting her wishes about her body, her weight, and her mental illness was not without drama. Colleen had moved in with Chris around the first of the year, and I had less contact with her. I was no longer visiting her on Saturday mornings. Her new home was about forty minutes away, in a direction I never traveled. I worked full-time, so I would have been able to visit only at times when Chris was also likely to be home. Colleen remained resolute in her determination to keep both Joe and me separate from Chris. So I stayed away. She had someone else to look after her now. She was twenty-four years old and in a relationship. I was glad to step aside and let her figure out her life with the help of a partner rather than with my help.

On a Saturday morning that April, I received a phone call from Carrie, my close friend and Colleen's former ballet teacher. Carrie had just gotten off the phone with Sophia, Colleen's ballet friend whom she had also tutored in math. Sophia had seen Colleen the night before in the audience of a professional ballet performance in New Hampshire. Colleen had been unable to get out of her chair without Chris's help. She was extremely thin and clearly quite weak. Sophia was alarmed and called Carrie to see what she knew.

Listening to Carrie, I felt my body entering crisis mode, an all too familiar state. I am good in a crisis, in that I think clearly, figure out first steps, and act, but I also experience a heightened nervous system response. My muscles tighten, I lose my appetite, and I feel a bit like I have had too much caffeine. I called Colleen right away. I left a voice message, but it was a couple of hours before I received a call back. During that time, I leapt to mentally planning how I could begin to get Colleen into a hospital. Her situation sounded dire, and I immediately assumed I would be intervening, as in the past. I thought about how I would need to involve Chris. He would have to be on board. I had no contact information for him, but I found him on Facebook and sent a message. I told him Colleen could not get well without help. I was not all that hopeful that he would see this private message, as it appeared that he rarely, if ever, used Facebook. I decided I would call him at work on Monday morning, if I did not hear back from him over the weekend. I also emailed and texted Colleen during those two hours of feeling desperate to connect with her.

When I eventually heard from her, she was apologetic. She knew it was a big deal for me to be worried about her and not be able to make contact right away. Colleen explained that she had been exercising and had not received my messages immediately. I had said and written simply that we needed to talk, but she heard and read my urgency and knew what I wanted to talk about.

Colleen did not hesitate to fill me in, once I told her what I had heard. She told me about not being willing to eat in front of

Chris, which had led to her not eating at all on weekends after moving in with him. She and he had had a conversation about this problem on a Saturday night in March, three months or more after she had moved to his place. They had come up with a plan for when she could eat on weekends, during times he was away from the house. The weekend eating would start the next day. But they were late with this plan, as he woke to find her unresponsive the next morning. He called 911. First responders revived Colleen from her low blood sugar state and moved her by ambulance to a local hospital. She was then moved again to a larger hospital an hour or so north. She was admitted to a medical unit, where her health was monitored over her five-day stay, with Chris bringing her food from home each day. She would not eat the hospital food. She insisted on eating the very limited diet that she weighed and measured, but she ate more than she had been.

Chris took that week off from work, and then the following week as well. She was considered a fall risk, so she needed someone with her at home after being discharged. A psychiatric stay for anorexia was strongly recommended but she refused that. She left treatment against medical advice.

This had all happened a few weeks before we spoke in April. She had kept it all a secret from me. No longer under my watchful eye, she had not heard from me that week she was in the hospital, so it was easy to keep me in the dark. This was her right. But now she was very concerned about all the medical bills that were arriving. She had not used her insurance benefits because she was still on our plan, and she had not wanted me to know about this hospitalization. She was clearly done with our opinions about how she should manage her health. It was at that moment that I began to understand I had done all I could to influence Colleen in this area of her life. We talked about the bills and agreed that she would send them all to me right away. This was an easy fix, as the hospitals and ambulance services were happy to charge our insurance company when I telephoned them. Realizing that I would no longer be able to keep Colleen from circling the drain of her mental illness was a bigger deal for me. While I recognized that all I had done over so many years to influence her to choose a healthy lifestyle had brought us to this point where she was clearly choosing anorexia, I also felt a huge sense of loss. My daughter had given up a battle that I had helped her fight, with varying success over many years, and there wasn't a thing I could do about her choice.

Did I feel guilty that April about not having been in closer touch with Colleen since her move to New Hampshire? Did I regret not having seen her as she was losing so much weight again? I did not. My new-found detachment from her health situation had been hard won. I had been ready for a breather. She was an adult, living with another adult, and I had been happy to let them carry on without my oversight. I did not later second guess my detachment over those months. I was a bit surprised to realize how little I had known about what was going on, particularly that she had been in a hospital. But I did not blame myself for this. Being in touch is a two-way street, and she had rarely reached out to me during that time either.

I focused my energy on helping Colleen by getting her medical bills paid. Taking over this task was time consuming, but not emotionally draining. It felt good to be able to do something for her, to help her in a tangible way. Over the following year I would gradually come to understand that my daughter would not live to see age thirty. But that spring, as she was turning twenty-five, I had enough to adjust to as I learned how and what she ate (only expensive protein powders purchased online and measured in precise amounts, calculated in response to her exact weight that morning) and how she exercised (gentle stretching to begin to build strength back after that hospital stay, later working up to exactly two hours a day of walking indoors). Letting go of any hopes that Colleen would recover from anorexia was enough for me to manage, without fully taking in just how short her life would be.

I wondered how Chris managed her intensity, her rigidity, her delusional thinking about her body, but I had no way of knowing his perspective on any of this, having still not met him. Joe was, as always, a good listening ear. He offered emotional support to me, simply by nature of being Colleen's other parent and therefore being deeply affected by all that went on with her. We shared our fears. But I continued to be the one on the front line of helping her. It was me she was willing to talk to. It was me who had more experience navigating the health care system and the financial and insurance systems I would need to help her with a year later. It was me, once again, offering her the support she needed.

When Colleen was twenty-two and still living at home, doing well enough in maintaining her weight, working at a job she loved, and spending time with Chris, I began to write our story. I wrote just a few paragraphs and decided it was too soon. She was too young, not yet far enough away from her adolescence and most recent hospitalization, for me to write about her. She wouldn't be ready for me to do this, and I felt I needed her permission to put pen to paper in this way. I wanted to write about her overcoming anorexia, along with my story of parenting her throughout those difficult years. You see, she was to live and do well. This is what I had still hoped and planned for. By the time she was approaching her twenty-fifth birthday, much had changed. I thought then that I would never write about us. I would not have a survival story to tell, so I would not tell our story. It was not until I began to write stories about my own childhood, three and a half years after Colleen's death, that I realized I could write about being her mother, about how I was affected by loving and losing her. I began to realize that I could explore in writing what this part of my life has meant to me, how I was changed by supporting this girl in the various ways I did. I began to see that I might tell the story of my pivot from helping her to survive to helping her to finish out her life in the way she chose.

27

Anticipating the Inevitable

COLLEEN NEEDED A LOT OF HELP from me from the winter of 2016 through to the end of her life in November of 2017. She had saved a large portion of her earnings when she worked at Omega Optical and, despite having not had an income for over a year, she had managed to make her savings stretch a long way. Living rent-free with Chris really helped. But in 2016 she was beginning to run out of funds and needed some income. She was way too frail physically, and emotionally debilitated by her obsessive-compulsive symptoms, to do any sort of paid work. I embarked on the cumbersome journey of helping her to apply for Social Security Disability Insurance.

While jumping through many challenging hoops of navigating a system that Colleen could not manage on her own, I was also dealing with feelings related to accepting what was inevitable and letting go of what I had once thought ought to be. It was no longer my job to influence her decisions; my work was to accept what she had chosen (a drastically shortened life in the service of anorexia), and to help her live out her life as she chose. This was incredibly challenging for me, emotionally. The goal of raising a child is to see her take flight, into an adult life, not to watch her decline into an early death with so many unfulfilled dreams.

I tried writing. I thought this might help me with my sadness. I drafted my first version of the eulogy I would eventually read at Colleen's memorial service. My first sentences went like this and remained unchanged:

Our daughter Colleen was a very tenacious person. From birth, she seemed to know her own mind. She knew what she wanted, and she knew when she wanted it. This became her story, more and more, as she grew into the young woman who has left us.

I did this writing to come to terms with the truth of what lay ahead and with my many feelings about losing this girl I had fought so long to save. Putting my thoughts about Colleen's life into words was helpful, at least a bit.

As Colleen approached her twenty-sixth birthday that spring, I spent countless hours helping her to get health insurance. But first came the disability hurdle for income. This was an impossible process for someone who felt unable to even talk on the phone with a Social Security representative. Colleen was so dysfunctional by this point that she couldn't imagine a phone call with a person of authority. So I took this on for her. Each person I spoke with at the Social Security Administration insisted on speaking with her. They simply needed her permission to work with me on her application. She couldn't do it. This requirement seemed to me such a ridiculous way for them to ensure they had her permission. Couldn't anyone get on the phone and say they were her? In the end, that's what I did. I hated this pretense, but after weeks of a stalled process, there was no work around.

One day during that time, after a particularly frustrating phone call with someone at the SSA, I threw a telephone across the room in my office at work. My friend and colleague, Jill, whose office was next door, heard this and appeared in my open doorway.

"Are you OK?" asked Jill. She was visibly concerned. I was not usually so dramatic in my behavior.

"No, I'm not OK," I responded. And I explained to her what I was dealing with. She already knew some of it, and she empathized. I softened a bit. Empathy can go a long way with me when I am under stress.

I was frustrated and angry with the SSA. I was exhausted by all I was doing to no avail. And I wished that Colleen could have a simple, brief phone conversation with the authorities. She insisted she could not, but they insisted she must, regardless of my efforts to explain to them that her inability to talk with them was part of her disability.

I continued with my project of securing services for my disabled daughter. After many weeks of working through details, Joe and I drove to an office an hour and a half from home (rather than wait another several weeks for an appointment closer to us) and successfully put in Colleen's application. I had piles of documentation of Colleen's mental health struggles, including extensive assessment reports, letters from Nancy and Colleen's psychiatrist, and three hospital discharge summaries. Many people I knew had warned me that Colleen's application would be refused the first time, as that seemed to be a common occurrence with the SSA. This is not what happened. I had asked Colleen for a current photograph to show how emaciated she was, and I had reams of paper that told her story and demonstrated that she would not be getting well, and that she would not live a long time. In the spring of that year, she was granted monthly SSDI payments. This was a huge win, but with her 26th birthday approaching, I needed to help her to find the medical insurance she would need when dropped from our plan on her birthday. Securing medical insurance for Colleen presented challenges as well, and I went through this process with her twice over the following year. There was a lot to navigate to prevent a lapse in coverage. Again, due to her level of dysfunction, I did it all. I am the one who gets these sorts of things done in my family.

Finding income and health insurance for Colleen, including all the time I spent on the phone with her, often felt like a full-time job. But I also had an actual full-time job and, even more challenging, all my feelings about the end of Colleen's life approaching. My grief connected to this inevitability was immense. In addition to writing that first draft of a eulogy for her, I met with Nancy a couple of times. Nancy offered some much-needed support but ultimately did not feel she could meet regularly with me because she had made a commitment to Colleen years before that she would always remain available to her, should she want to meet again. I understood this. Nancy offered me some names of other therapists I might meet with, each of whom I knew too well as former colleagues. Ultimately, I found that my two meetings with her were all I needed.

During those last couple of years of Colleen's life, I dealt with a wide array of feelings, including deep empathy for her. I empathized as she answered extremely detailed questions for me about how she spent every moment of her day. This was for the long SSDI application. I told her I would not comment, just record, as it was important to communicate an exact picture of her disability. I knew she would be hesitant to tell me the details unless I promised not to comment. Despite all I knew about Colleen's limitations, I was nonetheless shocked at the extent of her dysfunction. I was true to my word and said nothing to her about this. Her eating disorder consumed her life. She spent nearly every waking moment thinking about and managing her caloric intake, her weight, her exercise routine. She spent hours shopping online for deals on the awfully expensive protein powders that made up her diet. She had her food shipped from as far away as Australia. We spent a couple of long sessions on the telephone to get that exceptionally long questionnaire filled out. It was clear to me that her symptoms were growing worse all the time. She was imprisoned by anorexia, led there by her OCD. I ached for her.

I sometimes felt exhausted by the demands of supporting Colleen, and I sometimes felt resentful. Frustration and anger with the process of dealing with social service agencies was also significant. I felt frustrated with Colleen for not being able to take on any of this. I was back in the role of mother and advocate. I often felt strong and capable when advocating for her, but sometimes I was so tired of it all. I would come home from work in dire need of a quiet evening, only to remember that Colleen and I had scheduled a phone call. Our calls often felt endless. Her OCD led to going over things we had already said, multiple times. Sometimes I became impatient with her, in my fatigue and need for a break. But mostly I ached for her, for all she had lost, all the possibilities she had lost. And I felt deep sadness about all I was losing in watching her decline.

Sometime during the last couple years of Colleen's life, I told her that I couldn't handle seeing her, that I was as willing as ever to support her over the telephone but that seeing how emaciated she had become was too hard for me. We saw each other rarely but, when we did, I found her appearance too heart-wrenching to bear. She had for a long time been a beautiful girl, and now she was clearly starving to death. Not a good look, to say the least. Despite my knowing where all this was leading, that visual reminder of her impending death was more than I was willing to deal with. My moratorium on being in Colleen's presence did not last forever, just a half year or so. I softened on this, after some months, realizing I needed to see my daughter who would not be around in a few years.

I finally met Chris that spring. Joe and I were on our way to an Easter brunch at a friend's home, and Colleen and Chris were on their way to the same at his parents' place. We had arranged to meet in the food co-op parking lot to pass to Colleen her income tax return, filled out by Joe. I was certain she would be planning to approach our car alone on foot, but I made sure we arrived early so I could quickly approach the passenger side of his car before she had a chance to get out. I wanted to meet Chris. He was driving, of course, as Colleen had never learned to. I had a small gift for her and remained focused on giving both that and the tax forms to her. Chris and I simply said hello, but we had a warm non-verbal exchange. He had a kind face. I attempted to convey my appreciation to him, with my expression, and I was glad that he could finally see for himself that I was a good person. We exchanged what felt to me like warm and knowing glances as I talked with Colleen. This meant a lot to me, to finally lay eyes on Chris, to feel that he was not judging me, and to see for myself that he was a good guy.

In late May of 2016, my every-other-year teaching gig in the Netherlands came around again. This time, I did not have to worry about my mother dying; that had already happened, five months earlier. I was, however, concerned about what might happen to Colleen while I was away. Still, I went to Europe to teach for three and a half weeks, followed by an eleven-day vacation in Ireland with Caitlin. I was away from home for six weeks, after a long, grueling few months of helping Colleen with all that she could not manage alone. This trip gave me a break from constant awareness of Colleen's situation.

I knew I was going to lose Colleen, but I didn't know when. That year? The following year? Traveling felt risky; what if she died while I was teaching abroad? Who would take over the course? What if Caitlin and I had to cut our trip in Ireland short? What would it be like for me to lose her when so far from home? And yet it didn't make sense to put other aspects of my life on hold. Not knowing how long Colleen had to live added an additional layer to my grief around the inevitability of losing her. And I needed to keep living my life.

Sometime that summer, Colleen told me that her relationship with Chris had changed from what it had been when she had moved in with him eighteen months earlier. Chris remained a supportive friend and housemate, but the romantic nature of their relationship had ended not long after her hospital stay in 2015. He had figured out that Colleen would not be getting well. A year later, in 2017, she would tell me that he had begun asking her to find another place to live during the summer of 2016, but she did not tell me that then. She only told me that they were no longer as close as they had been. This did not surprise me, but it saddened me. I had felt a similar sadness when Colleen had been eighteen and developed feelings for her friend Josh. They had become close that summer, but she could not allow for touch. I once noticed him playing with the ends of her long hair while they talked on our porch. That was as much physical closeness that she, with her body image issues, could tolerate. When Josh went away to college that fall, he found a girlfriend whom he eventually married. Colleen felt crushed when he first got involved with that young woman. Once again, her OCD and eating disorder had gotten in the way of another important aspect of her life. Her social losses were hard for me to witness. Colleen lost so much to anorexia, which in the end ruled all her decisions and was of greater importance to her than anything else in her life. Here, again, her commitment to being thin had been more important than her relationship with Chris.

Over the last couple of years of Colleen's life, she saw friends less and less. She did stay in touch with Sophia, through reading her blog about living with anxiety and offering support of her writing. When she died, she had not seen her friend Kati for a few years, despite often visiting New York City where Kati lived and wrote. Once or twice, I suggested that Colleen contact Kati when she was going to the city for ballet performances, but she told me it was hard for her to see friends who were moving into adulthood so successfully. She was embarrassed by not working. She was focusing all her energy on exactly how many calories to eat and how many steps to take to burn those calories each day. This project consumed all her time, while her friends were pursuing graduate degrees, writing plays, and running marathons. Colleen was embarrassed by the choices she had made, but she saw no way out of those decisions. She felt powerless in the face of her mental illness.

In the spring of 2017, my sister-in-law, Cynthia, was in a life changing accident. Body surfing in Hawaii, she was dropped onto the beach by a rogue wave. Her neck was broken, and she became quadriplegic. This was an enormous tragedy not just for her, but for her family, her extended family, and her close friends. As not just a sister-in-law but also a long-time close friend of Cynthia's, since before we married brothers thirty years earlier, I became extremely involved in managing her support. I managed a Go Fund Me and wrote daily posts on a Caring Bridge site. I also spent a lot of time visiting her in rehabilitation hospitals in Boston that summer. Not long after Cynthia moved home to Vermont in August, Colleen told me that she needed to find a place to live. Chris was losing patience with her not acting on this request, as he had begun bringing it up a year earlier. This was all news to me. Colleen said that she had been holding off telling me about this for months because she knew how involved I had been since April with Cynthia. This struck me as a level of maturity I had not seen in Colleen previously. I appreciated this new mutuality in our relationship. Before this, in our relationship, Colleen's needs had always come first for her.

That fall I was back to working on finding services for Colleen, housing this time. When she died that November, I had copies of five thick housing applications on my desk. I had known that finding subsidized housing would be challenging, but I did not know it would be impossible. It was another year before I heard from one of them. I never heard from the rest. Getting her onto the waitlists for those five places that fall involved hours on the phone. I needed to do much of this during my workday, and then I typically spoke with Colleen after arriving home from work. Then I always had more work to do, to compensate for lost time during the day for the Colleen Project. When we spoke in the evenings, we always addressed concerns about the housing search first (mundane issues such as her latest income figure for an application), but we talked about other things as well. Colleen always wanted an update on what was going on for Caitlin in her pursuit of her BFA in Dance, as well as anything I knew about the goings on at the Brattleboro School of Dance. She would tell me about her recent or upcoming trips to New York City to attend American Ballet Theater performances. I did not feel that these trips were safe for her to take anymore, but this was what brought her joy. Attending dance performances was what she lived for at this point. We were both always ready to move from the mundane topic of housing applications to the more relaxed and fun topics. We addressed the ways she could try to stay safe as she traveled, but we mostly talked about the performances she attended.

In October, Colleen took her final trip to the city for ABT's fall season. She sent her food ahead, as she had been doing for some time, to the hotel she always stayed at. She lodged directly across the street from Penn Station, where she arrived by train. She brought just a small, wheeled bag with her mini sized laptop and personal essentials. She took cabs to Lincoln Center for performances. Still, this well-rehearsed trip, which she had been doing alone several times a year, proved to be too much at this point in her life. She did not fall while in the city on that trip, which had happened once previously outside of Penn Station, but the trip was exhausting for her, and she never fully recovered from that level of fatigue and physical stress.

Her last trip to the city was five weeks before she died. In the upcoming weeks, she fell twice at home and did not have the strength to get up. Once she had to crawl a long way, which was a slow process for her, to get to her phone. Both times she called Joe. Both times, he left work and drove to Chris's house in New Hampshire to help her up.

Sometime in mid-November, Colleen asked me if I would be willing to go to the city with her on a day in March, to change her tickets for the spring ABT season. She did this each year on what was known as ticket exchange day. She always purchased her tickets as soon as they became available in the fall. However, that far ahead of the season, it was not yet known which of the company's principal dancers would perform each show, and this mattered to Colleen. On a set day in March, she could exchange her tickets for different shows, but this had to be done in person. She knew she would not be able to go down and back in a day alone, and she knew that Chris was done helping her with this sort of thing. I would be on my spring break from teaching on the date she gave me, but I questioned whether it made sense for her to be buying tickets at all that year.

"Colleen, I am not sure you will be alive by next spring for these performances. I'm not sure you will be alive in March for ticket exchange day."

"But this season!" she cried. "This season is going to be so good! I can't miss it!" I found this heartbreaking to hear.

I agreed to go to the city with her in March. I told her to go ahead and buy her tickets. I was feeling quite certain that she would not be attending those performances, but it was easy to promise that I would help her exchange her tickets if she were still around in a few months. It was easy enough for me to offer her some hope, even when I wasn't feeling any of that anymore.

28

Good-Bye, Sweet Girl

COLLEEN AND I COMMUNICATED BY TEXT, not just by phone, in the summer and fall of 2017. Sometimes our messages were about her housing applications. Often, we messaged about setting up a time to talk. In one message, I see I was offering to pay an outstanding medical bill for her. Sometimes, our text messaging was more fun than all of that.

Thursday, July 27, 2017

Colleen: We just saw a bunny outside the house . . . I didn't know we had wild bunnies around here!
Me: Now you too! Caitlin sends me photos and videos of bunnies all the time, most recently yesterday. No fair!
Colleen: Just deer and woodchucks for Mom . . .
Me: Waa

Tuesday, November 7, 2017, 6:32 pm

Me: I am on the horn with Big C. Will call you when I get off this call.

This one, meant for Caitlin, was sent inadvertently to Colleen while I was talking with her. I like having a record of this, as I don't think I would have remembered that I sometimes referred to her as Big C. Clearly a joke between Caitlin and me. I am sure Joe was in on it as well. Caitlin says it originated from a Dr. Seuss alphabet book. *Big C, little c, what begins with C?* I think we held onto it with irony in Colleen's last years when she was so tiny.

Monday, November 20, 2017, 2:07pm

Colleen: Pictures? Oh, are you talking about picture options on your phone for text messaging?
Me: Yes, emojis. But I like calling them little pictures because that's what you called them once.
Colleen: I did—I've always thought emoji was a strange word. By the way, if you decide to bring up the possibility of the Nutcracker on December 20th with Caitlin, tomorrow, mention that Sarah Lamb will be Sugar Plum, with Steven McRae as her cavalier.
Me: Good to know. I did send the idea to her by text yesterday. She and I will discuss in person tomorrow. I am off to teach now.

Caitlin was to be home the next day for her Thanksgiving break. She was a senior in college. Colleen had suggested the three of us attend a ballet performance together in New Hampshire at Christmastime. I was hoping to make that happen, although I was holding off on buying tickets until talking to Caitlin. We didn't end up attending that performance, as Colleen died before then.

Monday, November 27, 2017, 10:51pm

Colleen: We are leaving Winchester now.

This was our last communication, by text. Chris was driving her over so she could go to bed and not wake up, here with us.

But these last examples of our text communications catapult us ahead to her last week. Between her final trip to the city in mid-October and her death a few days after Thanksgiving, there were those falling incidents which she needed Joe's help with, and there were conversations between Colleen and me about what she could expect next. Not long after purchasing those ABT tickets for the following spring, she began to wonder how long she would live. Perhaps my comments in our conversation about exchanging tickets influenced her thinking. One evening on the phone, about two weeks before she died, she expressed her frustration with her weakened state and the discomforts of living in such an emaciated body. She said she wished she knew how long all of this would go on. This life she was living had become quite uncomfortable physically and she wondered how long she would have to endure this pain. She was, for the first time, directly acknowledging that she knew she didn't have much time left.

"Colleen, you are in charge here, as you always have been. If you decide living is too painful and you are ready to go, all you will need to do is stop eating altogether. You are so low in weight that it won't take more than a day or two." I was standing by a bookcase in the entry to our living room. This fact is relevant only in that my memory of this conversation is so etched in my mind that the place I stood is synonymous with the words I spoke.

"You won't try to stop me?" she asked.

"Oh, Colleen, that ship sailed a long time ago. You know that. I haven't tried to stop you in years."

"OK," she answered meekly.

She seemed to appreciate that I was giving her permission to take charge of the end of her life. It seemed she needed to be reminded that I was on her team, supporting her choices to the end. These things were important for her to hear. I was her mother, but also her advocate and supporter. She was closer to me than to anyone else in her life at this point.

As for me, I felt good about my ability to talk to Colleen in this way. I had not planned to offer her my thoughts about how she might hasten her death. I don't believe I had even thought about her choosing to no longer eat at all, to end her life. But, in that moment, listening to her talk about not knowing how long she might live and suffer, I offered her an alternative, and this felt like a gift from me to her.

We ended our call, and I told Joe what had been said. I suspected he had heard my end of the conversation from where he sat in the dining room, but I wanted to make sure he knew all of it.

"Can't she just eat more?" he asked, in frustration.

"Oh, Joe, how can you suggest that at this point?" Clearly, he was exasperated. And I was tired, very tired. We both felt helpless. I believe his question came from not wanting to also feel hopeless.

I had known for a long time that Colleen would not get well. I didn't want her traveling to the city anymore, due to my concerns about all that could go wrong there. We had taken to her texting me once she arrived at her hotel, once she arrived at the theater, and again when back in her hotel. She knew now, weeks after that last trip, that she really couldn't travel alone again. She might not be able to travel even with help. Her weakened state, as evidenced by those falls at home in the weeks after that October trip, seemed to indicate that she had not recovered from that travel. She had come back more fatigued than ever and had not regained her energy or strength. She was too underweight and malnourished to recover.

Colleen joined us for Thanksgiving, after not having done so for several years. We celebrated the holiday with our extended family in Putney. I visited Cynthia a few days before and talked with her about how terrible Colleen looked. I wanted her to know this and to warn her sons, Colleen's cousins, that her appearance would be drastically different than when they had seen her a few years earlier. Colleen had missed quite a few holidays with our family during the years she celebrated with Chris's family instead. As it turned out, when we arrived for Thanksgiving dinner, one of Colleen's cousins was so shocked and distraught by her appearance that he stepped outside to compose himself.

Other than her emaciated appearance, she was fine to have around. We have a family tradition of going around the table when we sit down for our Thanksgiving meal, so each person can share something they are feeling thankful for. This tradition is usually lighthearted, but that Thanksgiving was the first since Cynthia's devastating accident and emotions ran high. Nearly everyone wept as they spoke of being grateful for the strong family we have. When it was Colleen's turn, she spoke eloquently about how much she appreciated being so generously welcomed back. I knew she felt some guilt about not having been around the family for a few years. What none of us knew during that meal and afterwards was that this would be the last time anyone present, other than Joe and me, would see Colleen. While I did not know this at the time, I did know that Colleen was approaching the end of her life, and I felt grateful that she made the decision to rejoin the family that day.

One of her reasons for staying away had been that she had not liked being asked what she ate, a question posed to her more than once at holiday meals. She did not partake of the food we all shared, having eaten whatever meager meal she allowed herself each year beforehand or afterwards. It's best not to query people with anorexia about their diet, but not everyone knows that. She had found such questions challenging and shaming. She never really answered them. But now she was back at the table with us, and no one batted an eye at her not eating. It was obvious that she was a person who did not eat.

Colleen had trouble getting comfortable in the living room after dinner that evening. She was skin and bones and required many pillows when in a sitting or prone position. I think she was particularly uncomfortable, physically, from having already sat at the dinner table during our long meal. For a while after dinner, while others were cleaning up in the kitchen, I was alone with Cynthia and Colleen in the living room, adjusting pillows for each of them. As I did this, I recalled taking care of my mother during her last holidays with our family. I felt sadness at finding myself in this position again, with two people who I felt were way too young (Cynthia not even sixty) to be requiring such care. But I didn't dwell on this for long. There were pillows to adjust and there was conversation to be made and soon there would be games to be played when the others joined us. Colleen's situation was devastating for me, and I could not look away from it during this holiday; however, I was determined to do what I could to make both Cynthia and Colleen comfortable, both physically and emotionally. I suppose I was on autopilot, to some extent, in my role as helper during that time. This was how I managed to do all that was needed to help these people I loved. When I was alone, at the end of the day, I felt nothing but heartbreak.

I drove Colleen home earlier than I would have liked, largely because she knew that Chris would be waiting to help her to bed before he could go to bed himself. She was afraid he would be impatient with her for keeping him up late. When we arrived at his home he met us at that door with a kind expression and took over for me in helping her up the few steps to the house. I still didn't know Chris. I just had my positive impressions of him, from the few times we had briefly encountered each other.

On the Sunday morning after Thanksgiving, I was sitting on the floor of the study reconciling Colleen's health insurance statements with her medical bills when the phone rang. It was Chris. He wanted to know which hospital we wanted Colleen sent to by ambulance. She had been unresponsive that morning, and he had called 911. First responders had revived her and now needed to transport her to an Emergency Department.

Joe and I arrived ahead of Colleen at the ED of our local hospital. Just after she was brought in, Chris arrived. I was both a bit surprised and pleased to see him. I told him right away that we would be moving home with us, that we just needed until the following weekend to rearrange a room on our first floor. Colleen would not be able to handle the stairs to her former bedroom. I had a hospital bed lined up that we would move into what was currently our study, but we would need a few days to arrange to move it there. Chris appeared relieved to hear this. I had been thinking over the previous few days that we would need to move her home, that it was time for Chris to be able to hand her back to us. He had cared for her long enough. But I hadn't offered this yet. As soon as I saw him in that ED, I knew it was time, whether I wanted her home with us or not.

I spent the day with Colleen, as Chris and Joe left to do other things. I kept in touch with Joe by phone, and he returned later that day to take her home to Chris's place. During our time in the ED, a doctor came in to speak with her, wanting to know how she had gotten to this point. She asked for my help in telling the long story of her anorexia. Because we ended up spending the next day in the ED as well, my memory is foggy on what happened each day. I do know that at the end of that first afternoon, Colleen needed to sign a form to leave the hospital against medical advice. She wanted nothing to do with being admitted and fed. Emergency Department staff reassured her that she was welcome to return at any point.

Chris called again the next morning, just as Joe and I were preparing to leave the house for work. Colleen had been unresponsive again, and Chris was calling to say simply that she was on her way, by ambulance, to Brattleboro. Joe and I agreed that he would go to work, and I would meet Colleen at the hospital. Chris went to work as well.

There was a lot of down time in the ED that day. While Colleen lay in a hospital bed, I sat by her side preparing my afternoon class. It wasn't until about noon that I realized I needed to cancel it, that this would be an all-day affair. Intravenous fluids were offered to Colleen, which she refused out of her irrational concern about her weight. A doctor came in to talk with her. Late in the afternoon, a no-nonsense social worker came in and spoke in a frank way with Colleen. She strongly recommended hospital admission. She told Colleen that if she were to fall and break a femur, it would not heal. She told her that it was uncertain how healthy she could become, but her life could be saved if she were willing to eat under medical supervision. She answered Colleen's questions about what she would be required to eat and if the hospital staff understood re-feeding syndrome. This woman understood how dire Colleen's health was, had a good idea of what healing would and would not be possible at this juncture, and was completely honest with Colleen.

My daughter refused to be admitted. This did not surprise me at all. Colleen wanted nothing to do with going through that long healing process she had endured in Boston years earlier only to relapse, and she had long ago decided on her course with anorexia. She would not give it up. She chose to go home.

When we got to the car, we started talking about how to avoid another trip to the hospital the following morning. Neither of us wanted to spend another day in the ED, and yet how would the next day be any different than the two previous mornings? We came up with a plan that involved her testing her blood sugar level after eating. (Her routine was to get up after only four hours of sleep, to start calculating, measuring, and weighing her protein powders. She had been doing this for a long time. Those past couple of mornings had resulted in her passing out a few hours after eating.) She had a blood sugar testing device but needed strips for it. We stopped at a drugstore so I could pick them up for her. On our half-hour drive to Chris's house, we talked about her options. While I understood how close she was to the end of her ability to stay alive, I did not want to influence her decision. I had helped her to come up with the blood sugar testing plan, which called for her to eat more if her blood sugar was too low the next morning, because I felt it was my job to support the idea of living. I was trying to give her the space she needed to decide on her own whether that was what she wanted to continue to try to do.

"I don't know, mom. This just doesn't seem to be working anymore. And I'm so tired."

"I'm sure you are, honey. It's been a long day, after a long day yesterday. Perhaps you will feel differently in the morning. You have the strips now, so you have the option to follow this new plan. But you will decide what to do."

"I don't know. I don't know if I want to get up tomorrow and try this or not."

"You don't have to, Colleen. This is your life and your choice. You don't have to set an alarm to get up and eat. I don't think you will wake up if you do not set the alarm. I would be really surprised if you did."

"I just feel so isolated. I don't see any of my friends anymore. Chris and I are no longer close. I feel so alone now." She paused. "I feel close to you. I do feel close to you. I know you love me."

"I do love you, Colleen, and I don't want to lose you. But you need to do what feels right for you."

When we arrived at Chris's house, he was kind and welcoming. The three of us stood in his kitchen, as Colleen and I updated him about what had transpired in the ED and about our conversation in the car. I asked him if he would be comfortable with Colleen not waking up in his home, if that was what she decided on. With his arm around her, he said he could offer that. I told Colleen she could come home with me, or she could go to bed there. This was her choice to make. She still didn't know what she wanted to do about the next morning. So, rather than stand by while she perseverated, I told her that I was going to drive home, giving her the space to decide, without my influence, what she would choose. I told her she could call me if she wanted Joe or me to drive back to New Hampshire for her, to bring her home. The three of us agreed to this plan, and I left.

About a half hour after I arrived home, Colleen called. It was now an hour since I left her, and it was getting late, around 10:00. She said she still wasn't sure what she wanted to do. We talked for a short while and I advised her to set a time limit for this decision that night. I suggested she decide what to do by 10:30 and to call me then. I reminded her that this was just a decision about the next morning. If she decided to get up and eat and test her blood sugar, she could make a different decision the next night about the following morning.

She called me back a half hour later and said she wanted to come home to go to bed and not get up at our house. I asked if Chris might be willing to drive her over to carry her into the house and up the stairs, and he said he would. Once she had settled into her bed, theirs was a brief but teary good-bye. However much their relationship had changed in recent years, they had been important to each other for a long time. And he had been a very good caregiver to her, right to the end.

Often, we humans think we know what we need, when in fact what we want and what we need most are different. Colleen, for so many years, wanted to be in control of all aspects of her life, making unhealthy decisions to serve that need. However, in the end, it seemed to me that what she needed most is what we all need, love and connection. This came into focus for me as I drove her home that evening after our second day at the hospital. She talked about feeling lonely and got as close to telling me she loved me as she had since she was a child. More importantly, she told me she felt close to me and knew that I loved her. As heartbreaking as it was for me to hear how isolated she felt, I appreciated hearing that she felt my love for her. Hearing that I had provided love and connection for her offered me a bit of solace, in the face of all her losses. My sadness was immense during that conversation. I was heartbroken, once again, as she acknowledged her sense of isolation, and yet there was this important moment, this glimmer of her also acknowledging how I had helped her during this last phase of her life, how I had continued to love and support her. I think it was not until much later, when I looked back on that drive, that I realized the full extent of the gift she offered me with her appreciation of my love.

What I had wanted for so many years, for my daughter, was for her to grow into a happy, healthy adult. We raise our children in hopes they will move into adulthood in a positive way, not to watch them make choices that lead to early death. And yet, in the end, after pivoting from that earlier goal I had for her, to supporting her wishes for her life, I began to need something different. I didn't know that until after I had been granted it. I needed a mutual, caring, close relationship with Colleen, and that was what I experienced during those last months, weeks, and most of all, on that last night of her life.

29

One Foot in Front of the Other

A SPOUSE WHO LOSES A PARTNER IS A WIDOW. A child who loses her parents is an orphan. But what about a parent who loses a child? We have no name for this person. Is this loss too unthinkable to label? Parents have lost children throughout history, more frequently in the past than now, but this is still a common occurrence. Perhaps, we don't want to think about this type of loss long enough to give the experience a name.

Despite not having a label for my loss, friends, colleagues, and acquaintances showed up to express their condolences. By showing up, I mean that we received home cooked meals five nights a week, delivered by friends for nearly three weeks; flowers and plants delivered in person or by florists; one-hundred thirty-five sympathy cards in the mail; countless email messages; and several beautiful tributes to Colleen written by her friends on my Facebook page. My on-going experience of grief would become much more private, but that early support was prolific.

I had imagined, since writing that first draft of my eulogy for Colleen, that after Colleen died we would hold a memorial event, and many people would attend. Colleen knew a lot of people in our community. She had touched many lives, through her math tutoring and her ballet mentoring, through her many other activities while growing up in Brattleboro, and through working for a local company. Joe has lived here since he was thirteen and I since age twenty-five. We know a lot of people around here. But, as it turned out, I had no energy to organize a memorial. I am the organizer in my family. Extended family did not jump in; Cynthia's accident had been only seven months earlier, and her family was barely coping with all that they needed to manage daily.

So we waited until mid-December, when Caitlin's semester at college was over and my nephew living in Oregon could fly in and my nephew living in Philadelphia could arrive, to hold an intimate event in the living room of our relatives in Putney. It was just the Vermont contingent of our extended family, plus Chris, Carrie, and my close friend, Sarah. I read the eulogy I had begun to write almost two years earlier.

During those early weeks when meals were delivered, I rarely went out. Colleen had been gone two weeks already when I finally went to see Cynthia. We both began crying as I entered her bedroom.

"Oh, Ann, I am so glad you are here."

"And I am so sorry it has taken me this long to get to you, Cynthia. I have just had so little energy for leaving my house."

"I understand."

"And I imagine it's been hard for you to not see me."

"Yes, it has."

Cynthia sat propped in her bed, unable to move any part of her body below her shoulders. Cynthia, who had been one of the most physically active people I knew, before her accident. Cynthia, a beautiful vibrant person whose life had been changed so dramatically, but who remained as concerned about others as she was about her own life. She always wanted to hear what was going on for friends who visited her, even in the early months from a hospital bed.

Cynthia had loved Colleen. She had been a wonderful aunt to her as she was growing up, always interested in what was new with her, always offering to fix her long hair in yet another creative style. And she had been supportive to me throughout my years of dealing with Colleen's mental illness and final decline. I remembered her telling me that whenever she would learn that Colleen was not eating enough, again, she herself would lose her appetite. She loved her niece and felt helpless in the face of her struggles.

In the sixteen months that Cynthia lived beyond Colleen's death, she and I reminisced frequently about that girl my daughter had been. We smiled and laughed often about things Colleen had said and done. Joe and I did this too, as I did with Caitlin, but there were not many other people I shared memories of Colleen with. When Cynthia died, my loss was enormous—a dear friend of many decades, a companion in joining our husbands' family and then in raising our children as cousins, the sister I did not have growing up, and in the end a person who inspired many with the grace with which she dealt with her sudden and enormous disability. In addition to all of this, I lost one of the few people in my life who had not only known and loved Colleen since she was a baby, but also loved to talk about her with me.

During those first weeks after Colleen died, I gave myself permission to do whatever I wanted, or nothing at all. I was able to finish my last bit of grading for the semester from home. I didn't have to buy many groceries but, when I did, I tried to slip in and out of the store during quiet times of the day, so as not to run into people I knew. I didn't want to chat with anyone. I mostly just did what my calendar told me to do. When I showed up for a regularly scheduled haircut, my stylist was surprised to see me. "I am just putting one foot in front of the other," I told her. "Just doing what it says on my calendar." I also needed to go to the Department of Motor Vehicles that December, to have a new photo taken for my driver's license. The woman taking my picture said I could smile or not. I did not have a smile to offer the camera, so now I am stuck for years with a very grim photograph that reminds me of those early weeks after Colleen's death.

One foot in front of the other worked for me. Joe and I drove to Long Island just four days after Colleen died, to see Caitlin dance. Down and back in a day, a trip that Colleen had been hoping to take with us. One foot in front of the other. I texted Colleen's phone about the performance, while Joe drove us north on I-95 that night. I knew, of course, that she was dead, but I couldn't not tell her about the show she had missed, about how beautifully her sister had danced. I no longer recall the specifics of that show, or what piece Caitlin performed. I am not sure I could have recalled those details within a week or so. But I knew them at the time, and Colleen had always liked hearing the details. She would have loved that performance, and so I typed that to her phone from my phone. I didn't mention to Joe what I was doing. I thought it would sound crazy, and it was just a private moment. I took a brief break from staring ahead into the darkness to put some of my thoughts into words for Colleen.

I was fortunate to not have to return to the office and class-room until late January, due to the semester break. Joe went back to work that same week Colleen died. For him, one foot in front of the other meant going into the small office, with supportive colleagues, where he worked. Joe likes to work, and doing so at that time provided some distraction for him

It was the time of year when days are at their shortest. I liked a short day. A meal delivered by a friend after dark. An evening of I-don't-know-what, and then early to bed. All that darkness suited my mood. A friend at work, the one who had organized the meals, asked me months later how I had spent my days in those first weeks, and my only answer was that I couldn't remember. I know that I cleaned the house, responded to email, and did that final grading of my students' work. I may have read. I always read. Caitlin came home for her semester break. We celebrated our birthdays with a meal and dessert delivered by a friend. I don't remember much else. I don't think there was much else.

Joe and I got Colleen's ashes into the ground, alongside my mother's, just before the earth became too frozen to dig in early December. I read a poem by Ursula K. Le Guin. It was just the two of us, just before dark, on a cold, grey day, in a world of bare trees and fallen leaves, endings in the air. The two of us buried our daughter's ashes twenty-seven-and-a-half years after she was born to us on a beautiful sunny day in May, hope and renewal in the air. Bright, so bright, that day and her.

30

No Regrets

Grief is love.
Under the weight of grief lies light.
It seems that only those who grieve know grief.

THESE ARE THOUGHTS I find on my computer, thoughts that I wrote in the months after Colleen's death. I saved them in a document labeled simply, "Grief." I typed them in at different times.

A year or so after Colleen's death, I wrote:

Imagining loss seems easy enough for most people, imagining grief not so. So much empathy, from so many well-wishers after her death. Nothing now. I mention her name in conversation and there is no response. An awkward moment. No recognition that I have spoken. Very rarely is there any sort of acknowledgment that I had two daughters, that I have lost one, that I still grieve for my girl and always will. A former colleague says Colleen when she means to say Caitlin, I simply say Caitlin, and she apologizes profusely . . . like I shouldn't be reminded of Colleen, like it is a faux pas to say her name.

Grief is love, but it is also silent. Under the weight of grief lies a hint of light, sometimes.

As I now read these words, written a few years ago, another memory comes to mind. Colleen had been gone two years, maybe. I was lacing up my ice skates at the Retreat Meadows, a popular outdoor skating spot in Brattleboro. This place offers not just great skating but lots of opportunities to run into friends and acquaintances. Mollie, who had taught Colleen to skate through the Recreation Department in town, was sitting on a plastic milk crate not far from mine, lacing up her skates.

"Colleen loved learning to skate," Mollie said to me. I smiled, both at her mention of Colleen and at my memories of my girl on the ice.

"Colleen was serious about learning anything she took on, Mollie. That girl loved to learn."

"She was fun to teach," said Mollie, enjoying her memory. And I felt, in that moment, that even if the skating proved to be sub-par that day, I was glad to have gone down to the Meadows. Mollie remembered Colleen with fondness. While I knew this was probably true for many adults and young people across town and beyond, Mollie knew to tell me this. Her words made that day a better one for me.

Three months after Colleen's death:

I am the person I was when I was wishing for a daughter, and I am the person I was when I met her and raised her. I am the person I have always been, and I am more than I used to be. I was blessed with her. And I am better because of her. I learned to be patient. I deepened my understanding of compassion. I found love deep within myself that transcended frustration, anger, disappointment. I experienced many difficult emotions in my relationship with Colleen but love always prevailed.

May 14, 2020:

Here We Lie
Stretching out by the stone
That marks the place
Where light grey ash
Mingles with dark brown soil.
Playing with the stones Chris has left
On your thirtieth birthday.
Placing them in the grooves of your name,
You would have liked this game.
Blake said to kiss a joy as it flies.
Ursula said it is in the dark we grow souls,
That hope lies not from above, but below.
I hold you close, as I let you go.

Many people believe in an afterlife. I think this is helpful when losing someone. Grievers are comforted by their belief that the person they have lost exists, somewhere. I only know of this life. I don't know what happens afterwards. I do know that as I get older, my daughter stays twenty-seven. I always know what age she would be if she were alive, and she is also forever twenty-seven.

What has helped me the most in not crumbling under this terrible loss is the fact that I have no regrets. I did all I could do. I felt this way in her final years, as I was supporting her in a different way than I had previously, and I have felt this way since she died. I have not doubted the ways in which I parented my daughter. I was not a perfect parent, by any means. There is no such thing as perfect, after all—something I tried over and over to explain to Colleen, something she never could accept. I do know I did all I could to help her. Knowing that I did right by her comforts me as I move forward in my life with one adult daughter rather than two.

31

These Dreams of You: At the Beach

July 2022

Dear Colleen,

I am standing on the edge of the shore, gentle surf lapping over my bare feet. In and out, the waves ebb and flow, and I think of you by my side on this very beach when you were a girl.

I remember how we perched beside each other in beach chairs, watching the size of the islands change as the tide shifted, watching sailboats slow dancing across our view, watching cormorants diving and guessing where they might emerge. We delighted in the sandpipers as we walked the shore. We searched for starfish in the tidepools but released them back into their watery home after watching them wiggle in our palms. We talked about the changing light, and I told you about Monet's series paintings.

You were my buddy at the beach, Colleen. You and I spent hours identifying seabirds and seaweed and seagrass and sea creatures, adding a sticker with each discovery to the right spot in your seashore identification book. I see you sitting in a purple swimsuit, legs covered with a colorful beach towel, dark hair long and wet, summer freckles sprinkled over your pretty face. Gazing out to sea alongside me and studying your beach book, you enjoyed my company as much as I enjoyed yours.

I see you on this beach in Maine every year, Colleen. I see you returning from that miles-long walk to Camp Ellis and back, when I could not imagine you would go half that far alone when you set out. You wore that purple swimsuit and a beach towel as a skirt. There was always a skirt.

I see you here in Maine and at home in Vermont, everywhere I turn. You are still with me, Colleen. You will always be with me.

Acknowledgments

Thank you, Pam Bernard, writing teacher extraordinaire. Without your belief in the importance of this story and my ability to write it, I wouldn't have taken it on. Your guidance throughout my process was invaluable.

Thank you, Lyn Sperry, for reading early chapters and appreciating my writing style. Your suggested edits on my full manuscript helped clarify my story.

Thank you, Alison Scott, for your feedback and support throughout my writing process and for your extensive reactions to my manuscript.

Thank you, Dede Cummings of Green Writer's Press, for your enthusiasm in publishing my book and for your collaborative approach to design.

Thank you, Rose Alexandre-Leach, for appreciating my memoir and offering astute editing suggestions. I can't imagine working with a better editor.

Thank you, close friends of Colleen, especially Sophia Marx, Lena Serkin Mazel, and Kati Schwartz, for loving her. Thank you, Brattleboro School of Dance community, for all the support offered over the years and for continuing to honor Colleen through her annual memorial ballet class. Thank you, Carrie Towle, for your mentoring and appreciation of my daughter, for sharing with me your memories of certain events, and for honoring Colleen so beautifully every year as you teach her class.

Thank you, Nancy Kale, for all the help you offered to Colleen, me, and my family. Thank you for your dedication to her well-being and your appreciation of her as a unique individual with admirable traits, not just mental illness.

Thank you, Chris, for all you did for Colleen.

Thank you, Sarah Waldo, for your unwavering support over the years. You were there for me from beginning to end, all twenty-seven-and-a-half years of Colleen's short life and again after her death.

Thank you, Joe Meyer, for your steadfast partnership in challenging times and all the fun we had in lighter moments as we raised our daughters together.

Thank you, Caitlin McCloskey-Meyer, for sharing your perspective on parts of this story. You are my best buddy in remembering Colleen. I wrote this book for you above all others.

About the Author

ANN MCCLOSKEY holds an M.A. degree in Counseling Psychology and a B.A. in Social Work. She spent two decades training clinical mental health counselors in a graduate program at Antioch University, while also working as a licensed clinical mental health counselor. She subsequently spent fourteen years teaching psychology at a small college serving students who learn differently. With her husband, Joe Meyer, Ann raised two daughters in rural Vermont. This is her first book.

Printed in the USA
CPSIA information can be obtained
at www.ICGtesting.com
CBHW031248210923
1042CB00005BA/9